FROM THE CULT
TO THE KINGDOM

DUBB ALEXANDER

FROM THE CULT TO THE KINGDOM

DUBB ALEXANDER

First Paperback edition October, 2021

Cover design by Lisa Von De Linde,
LisaVdesigns.com

Cover photo by Samuel Kilgore,
pagesofsamuel.com

Manufactured in the
United States of America

Scriptures referred to in this book are taken from the most up to date translations of the Holy Bible published by Zondervan Publishing House and provided online by biblegateway.com.

Published by Victory Vision
Publishing and Consulting
victoryvision.org

PAPERBACK ISBN: 978-1-7378734-0-2
EBOOK ISBN: 978-1-7378734-1-9

DEDICATION

I dedicate this book to King Jesus,
without Whom, there is no Kingdom.

To my beautiful wife, Beth, and my amazing
daughter, Cinda. Without your support, I could
not have accomplished any of the things that
matter. Y'all are my favorite!

To Mark and Cinda Urquhart. Thank you for
choosing to trust and invest in me before I
deserved it. Without you, I would not be the man
that I am today.

To all the Prophetic Kingdom Reformers out
there who are ready to change
culture by advancing The Kingdom.
Christ in YOU is the hope of the world!
I love you all.

CONTENTS

	Acknowledgments	i
	Foreword by Dan McCollam	iii
	Preface	vii
1	Gangster's Paradise	1
2	The Bad News	9
3	Cult Life	17
4	From Bad to Worse	27
5	A Fresh Start	37
6	Flat and Yellow	43
7	Never Ask Me Again	53
8	Original Intent	67
9	The Heresy Hunters	77
10	Remantled for Government	87
11	Fathers Add Value	95
12	Place of Pain, Place of Reign	103
13	Confirmation and Credentials	113
14	School of Kingdom	121
	Bibliography	124
	About the Author	125

ACKNOWLEDGMENTS

Thank you to Dan (Dano) McCollam for
championing me, and for all the wisdom
that you continually lend me.

Thank you to Julie Ballard for walking me through
getting this project done and making it available
to the masses.

Thank you to all my #Kingdomcomrades who
always encourage me in my Kingdom exploits.

Thank you to all the staff and students in the
School of Kingdom whose passion and progress
breathes life into my assignment.

FOREWORD

After traveling six continents, connecting with thousands of amazing people, and writing a couple dozen books, I'm at that ripe age and station in life where I receive a budding author's foreword or endorsement request just about every month. It's as if someone signed me up for a new author's book-of-the-month club. Remembering the good old days of being a new author, and still learning myself, I try to read and serve as many as I can. This book is different. I requested this book.

A little more than a year ago, Dubb Alexander sent me his first book manuscript. I originally knew Dubb as a friendly guy who showed up over-dressed at my training conference. It wasn't that awkward, "Why didn't someone tell me this was a casual wedding?" type of over-dressed; Dubb just outclassed the room with a crisp business suit. Most of us at the conferences were clad in California-casual jeans and a button-down, while Dubb looked like he had just come from the White House. Little did I know, at that time, that this description leaned close to the truth.

So, the manuscript Dubb originally sent me featured some great theological points and dashes of rap-like poetry, seasoned with tiny biographical bits from his life story. I enjoyed it all, but I found myself craving more of the flavors of this crazy story. I called Dubb on the phone and said something like, "This isn't a good book, (shocked silence on the other end) it's three good books! Would you consider dividing this material into three books, starting with an elaboration on your personal story?" In his typical gracious style, Dubb agreed. Now we have this unbelievable, but true, account of a child raised in the projects, inducted into a cult, who finds true faith, and grows to stand before world leaders.

From the Cult to The Kingdom is a book about many things. It's a brief expose' on the loneliness and fatherless atmosphere often found growing up in a violent, low-income neighborhood. The story moves geographically and thematically as Dubb shares his journey, first pulling back the curtain on weird rituals, practices, and abuses found on the inside of some of today's religious cults. Escaping the cult, our next stop in Dubb's journey challenges our views on evangelism, why Jesus had to die, and the very nature of God. But the final stop in this journey is this book's intended end—the liberty and dignity that comes from seeking first the Kingdom of God and His righteousness.

So, join us on this fascinating journey with prophet, trainer, statesman, and author, Dubb Alexander. We will travel the road together from cultic confusion to a kingdom-revelation that revolutionized the life of one man and is now touching the lives of thousands. Don't be surprised if you find parts of his story strangely relatable. I believe that in Dubb's journey, you just might find an upgrade for your own.

Dan McCollam is an American author, trainer, and co-founder of the Prophetic Company and Bethel School of the Prophets. His books include Bending Time, Finding Lost Things, Basic Training in Prophetic Activation, and The Good Fight.

PREFACE

The late, great, South African Prophet Kim Clement was famous for saying, "Your place of pain shall become your place of reign!" I have found no other prophetic promise to ring truer in my life.

From bearing the soul-wounds of a father who was a cult leader to being used mightily by The Lord to provide a clean slate for a nation which bore the soul-wound of a cult, I hope that my story will make it clear and apparent to you that whatever has come against you without your permission can be so redeemed by your Good Father that it will ultimately become the very weapon with which you will do great violence to the system of darkness.

If King Jesus can walk me out of my impoverished existence in the hood of south Dallas, lead me through the maze of abuse in a cult in Waco, Texas, and ultimately seat me at tables with various heads of state around the world, where I may serve Him as a mouthpiece and share the strategies of Heaven with the kings of the earth so their people might experience the goodness of God, then what will He do through you?

CHAPTER 1
GANGSTER'S PARADISE

I grew up in South Oak Cliff, a neighborhood in downtown Dallas, now being gentrified to conform toward the middle-to-upper class homeowner. However, in the 80s and 90s, it was "the hood."

In our tiny house, I was awakened on countless nights by the sound of gunshots within blocks of us—from and in—any given direction. Occasionally, the gunshots were followed by the wail of sirens, or perhaps the whirl of helicopter blades and the sweep of a searchlight across my window if a particularly heinous crime had occurred. During blazing hot summers, it was common to see drug deals being made between hustlers and sweaty patrons on the street corner. Street gangs were prevalent, making street justice the governing authority of the area.

Street smarts for the lone white family in the hood meant keeping one's head down, and never making eye contact with anyone who was not from the same block. I was the fifth child of ten, born at home in our broken-down suburb to two atheist hippies. My parents did not believe in God, or even acknowledge the existence of a god. They were anti-establishment in every way, which resulted in their ineffectively taking on the roles of sole health care and educational providers to my siblings and me. Having created an awkward bubble of isolation, my parents, and we ten children, existed in the midst of a violent and greed-driven society.

Born at home with the assistance of a midwife, the umbilical cord was wrapped around my neck three times, and I entered this world gray and lifeless. My parents were forced to call an ambulance to rush me to the hospital, where thankfully, I was resuscitated, but I suffered from nocturnal seizures the first few years of my life because of complications from my birth.

Our first home in Oak Cliff, a small, white, two-bedroom house with a tiny front porch, was on the Hispanic side of town. My father had put plywood boards down the center of one of the bedrooms and placed the boys on one side and the girls on the other. The tight quarters and single bathroom meant no privacy for anyone. Poverty was my normal and only life experience. Apart from the rare occasion when a box of Jiffy cornbread was mixed with water and baked into a brick-shaped, sadly disappointing forgery of the picture displayed on the packaging, rice and beans were the only food on the table, twice a day.

On unbearably hot days, my siblings and I trudged around the tiny living room in a small circle, savoring the few seconds when we would be the one to walk past the swamp cooler that hung loosely in the back window. We leaned in as we passed by to get as close as possible to the slightly cooler, moist flow of mildewed air that brushed past our faces.

On the rare occasions that we ventured outside of the house, we either walked to nearby Kiest Park or the Hampton Illinois Public Library, or once a week we rode in our once silver, then rust-colored, cutlass station wagon down the oak-lined streets to the Sack & Save grocery store. Although Oak Cliff was a part of the well-known city of Dallas, each neighborhood on the south side operated as its own island, seemingly a world away from the rest of the celebrated city. There was rarely a need for us to travel outside our three-square-mile realm of existence; everything we needed was within walking distance. Looking back, it is still odd to me how secluded our neighborhood was from the rest of the metropolis.

3

My father was a clock repairman by trade and worked from home, training each of his children to work in the family business as we got old enough to take responsibility for the simpler tasks. There was always at least one wall, and multiple tables in our house, covered by dozens of ticking clocks, and one can imagine the cacophony of chimes that broke out at the top of every hour. I often sat on the tire swing that hung from the lone tree in our small, chain-link fenced backyard, simply to escape the incessant ticking, which served as a dismal reminder of my perpetually mundane existence.

I was made for people! For connection! For adventure! And yet all three were painfully absent from my life.

Once every five weeks, it was my turn to ride with my parents to a little clock shop in the north side of Dallas, where my father returned the clocks he had repaired that week. He then picked up a new batch. from a little clock shop in the Olla Podrida Mall. In retrospect, it was probably only a thirty-minute ride, but seeing something new outside of the three-square miles that dictated every aspect of the rest of my life made the ride feel like three hours.

When I was seven years old, my mother and I set out on an uncommon excursion to Oak Cliff

Donuts, to get breakfast for our family to celebrate my father's birthday. It was a rare treat, and I was excited to be the one chosen to go with her. After making our purchases, we stepped out of the pastry shop back onto the blacktop parking lot, only to be met by a violent string of loud obscenities cutting through the muggy air. Two men were arguing at the bus stop just a few feet away, and before I could even grasp what was taking place, a cadence of gunshots rang through the air, and one of the men dropped to the ground right before my eyes. I had just witnessed my first murder—on the streets that I called home.

As our family grew in number, our tiny two-bedroom became increasingly insufficient and could no longer hold our growing family within its crowded walls. My grandparents had recently evacuated their long-time family home on the black side of Oak Cliff near the Big T Plaza. It was offered to us as a residence, so we moved our large family just a few blocks away, across Five Mile Creek, which ran next to the Skaggs Alpha Beta grocery store. The culture was radically different, but the crime rate was comparable; although they rode under names, colors, and symbols that were unfamiliar to my ever-watchful eyes, the same type of gang structure dominated the area.

The alley behind our new home boasted basketball goals in every driveway. I found that playing basketball with my new friends was a way to escape the lack of privacy in my home. Even though my quick wit and humor made me more welcome than my ball-handling skills, I was free to be me on the courts. It was here that I fell in love with the music, blasting from boomboxes sitting curbside, a style of music I had never heard before. They referred to it as "hip-hop."

Unfortunately, the good times were constantly overshadowed by a foreboding sense of fear. My mother was robbed at gunpoint coming out of the Skaggs Alpha Beta grocery store one evening. It evoked anxiety in us all, because unlike the few more fortunate in the neighborhood, we could not afford bars on our windows and doors. Inside my mom's stolen purse were the keys to our home, and our address on her ID. I will never forget stacking furniture up against the doors and windows so that we could feign some semblance of security as we attempted to engage some level of rest for the night. The lengths to which gang bangers in our neighborhood would go for selfish gain were not to be taken lightly, regardless of the motivation behind their actions, whether for survival or worse, a game of greed that they played to win.

It would be a lie to say that I ever felt truly secure drifting off to sleep at night. Even the night air was dominated by loud bass lines, bumping from the trunks of lowrider cars filled with people looking to score their next hit. The dope runs went on all through the night and into the early dawn. Oak Cliff never slept.

Since we were "homeschooled," if one wanted to call it that, the only people I had any interaction with were my family, and the few neighborhood friends with whom I was offered the occasional, much sought after opportunity to play with from time to time. Rap and basketball were my places of retreat. However, escaping the attention of my parents to crash a friend's game was a hard task, and I would never think of rapping a freshly written sixteen bars openly at my house; that music was considered by my parents to be, "Not for us."

Occasionally on a rare outing, I caught a glimpse of the downtown Dallas skyline from the intersection of Polk and Highway 67. I would look around at the trash that littered the streets and parking lots—a prime example of what it looks like when there is no community pride—and wonder about the people in those tall buildings that seemed worlds away. What were their lives like? Surely, they did not have to watch their backs every moment of every day. What kind of homes did they live in? What did they do for a living? Did they ever stare back at my part of town from their corner offices in the sky?

Although dreaming for bigger things was not a concept taught within the framework of my constricted existence, I somehow knew, deep down, that the meager hand of cards I had been dealt would most certainly play out the rest of my life in like-mundane fashion if I did not do something intentional to break free and break out of the familiar. Little did I know that before I would have a chance to make that move, things would get worse. The physical dangers of an existence in the hood were to become further complicated by the influence and manipulation of a cult that would soon extend an invitation, beckoning to my already dysfunctional family.

CHAPTER 2
THE BAD NEWS

The first time I remember being cognizant that a god might really exist was as a small child. It was Thanksgiving dinner at my grandfather's house. He blessed the food with an eloquent, poetic prayer in which he asked that, "The gracious, heavenly Father might continue to pour out blessing on everyone gathered at the table." I loved my grandfather deeply, and he seemed so sincere that I thought for the first time that maybe my parents might be wrong, and that perhaps, just perhaps, there might be a god after all.

As this truth dawned on me, I figured I might as well toss a prayer up myself. I will never forget my brilliant six-year-old's strategy coming to light in the simple phrase, "God, if you are real… I'm on your side." I was always one to hedge my bets. Outside of this experience, I never really thought about God until an encounter that resulted in my salvation experience five years later.

When I was eleven, we met another huge, home-schooled family that was also quite ill-adjusted to society. I became fast friends with two of the Smith brothers, James and John. All the children in this family intentionally bore biblical names, although at that time, I had no reference for such a thing. James and John flanked me in age, on either side, by a year. One day, James pulled me to the side and witnessed to me about Jesus, God, and Heaven. I could tell he was nervous, but his words came from the heart. Of course, he did the best he knew how as he introduced me to what I now call, "The Bad News."

The conversation in the backyard of their house in east Texas started like this, "Hey man, have you ever heard about hell?"

"No. What's that?"

"Well, we are all sinners, and that's where God sends us when we die."

"What's a sinner?" I inquired.

"We have done bad things, and those bad things make Him angry because bad things deserve punishment."

"So, hell is the place He sends you to be punished?"

James nodded solemnly. "It's a lake of fire that you fall in and keep on falling. You burn forever; it's pitch black."

I stared at James in shocked silence. I did not know much, but I knew this was not good. In fact, it was the most frightening thing I had ever heard, and I had witnessed some crazy stuff coming off the streets. I was also a little confused as to how I was finding myself in this predicament. I felt blind-sided and as though I had had very little say in the matter. Until five seconds before, I had been completely unaware that any of this was going on, and yet it seemed like so much hung in the balance of my ignorance!

James continued now with a glimmer of hope in his voice, "But if you ask Jesus to be your Savior, then when you die, you go to Heaven and live with Him forever!"

"My Savior?" I queried.

"Yes," James continued. "Jesus, God's Son, came to Earth and died on a cross, and His blood paid for your sin. He got punished for you. It is a gift! You just have to pray and accept it!"

"And what's Heaven again?" I asked curiously. I have always been one to want to know all the facts before I make a decision.

James looked up and pointed to the sky, "Well, it's up there, and you sit on a cloud and play on a harp and sing to God all day."

Now, one must remember that I was an eleven-year-old boy living in the hood of south Dallas; all I wanted to do was rap and play basketball. This cloud, harp, and singing destiny sounded terribly dull.

"All day?" I sought clarification.

"All day," James assured me.

My next question was, "For how long?"

"Well, forever, of course," James replied, clearly puzzled by my line of questioning. In his mind, he had just offered me the deal of the century, and my questions seemed needless in his eyes.

I carefully weighed the options: clouds, harps, singing. The celestial choir boy destiny was definitely not my jam, but it did sound slightly better than falling forever in a fiery darkness. "I guess I choose Heaven," I said to James' evident excitement.

Upon voicing my decision, James led me in the traditional sinner's prayer. I asked Jesus into my heart to forgive my sin and to take me to Heaven when I died. James then gave me a little white pocket-sized Gideon New Testament, with the bonus books of Psalms and Proverbs crammed onto its unbelievably thin pages, in the smallest font I had ever seen. That was the beginning of my journey with God.

That day, I was innocently introduced to a God who was angry at me because I was a sinner, a God who desired to throw me into a lake of fire because of my dirty, sin-riddled, human existence. I also learned that if I cashed in on the blood of His Son, whom this monster God had apparently murdered, that I would begrudgingly be allowed into a fluffy, cloud-filled eternity where I would spend forever plucking a harp and singing songs that were not even closely reminiscent of my favorite, carefully hidden cassette tape of LL Cool J. Not only had I been given a terrible mis-representation of the nature of my good, kind, and loving heavenly Father, but I had also completely missed out on why I was being saved. Many of us understand that we were saved from something, but we are unaware that we have been saved *for* something!

Another thing happened that day for which I had no language, reference point, or grid; it was a supernatural phenomenon that I would not understand until many years later. I began to dream dreams that would come true in meticulous detail. The first one that I can remember consisted of my picking up a book (that I was reading in real life), from the coffee table in the front room and continuing into the story past the point where I had paused the day before. As I came to the end of a chapter on a specific page, my mother rounded the corner and told me to go unload the dishwasher. A seemingly inconsequential dream, it would appear, until I found myself the next day picking up this very book and reading word for word the content which I had dreamed the book would contain the night before.

My mind struggled to comprehend what was happening as I came to the close of the chapter referenced in my dream the night before, and sure enough, my mother rounded the corner and informed me that it was indeed my turn to unload the dishwasher, and that she needed it done right away.

Of course, I now understand that this was the seed of the seer prophet that I would one day become beginning to wake up within me, but at the time, the only conclusion I could come to was that I might be going mad. An unreasonable fear that I might be sent to a mental institution took up residency in my mind, causing me to never share with anyone what was happening, even as the dreams became more frequent. The gifting progressed to the point that, while wide awake, I began to catch pictures in my mind of events right before they would play out before my eyes in the physical dimension. Whether it was a certain type of car turning onto our street, or a certain type of clock coming in for repair on a certain day, I never spoke of it.

Even though these dreams were the beginnings of my spirit man awakening to its divine design and gifting, I had no one to connect the dots for me and explain that this was in some way related to my newfound spiritual reality. So, I mostly tried to ignore it and began to build my relationship with Jesus based upon the only thing that felt real in my hands, the pocket-sized Gideon New Testament that James Smith had given me upon my profession of faith, along with his instructions to start with the Gospel of Matthew, and, for some reason, the epistle of James.

In the epistle of James, one verse in particular practically jumped off the page at me.

If any of you lacks wisdom, you should ask God, who gives generously to all without finding fault, and it will be given to you. (James 1:5 NIV)

I can still remember reading it for the first time and thinking, could it be that I had found a shred of certainty to hang onto during my chaotic existence? It was the simple prayer that a complicated boy, living in a constant state of uncertainty could wrap his mind around. I began to silently pray those very words every day; it became the most consistent thing in my life at that time. Little did I know that this introduction to some level of truth, and a developing friendship with wisdom, would rescue me from becoming a casualty to the events that were about to unfold in my life.

CHAPTER 3
CULT LIFE

S hortly after my encounter with the "bad news," the Smith family decided to court a cult in Waco, Texas. No, it was not the Branch Davidians, but only twenty miles across town. The two groups definitely shared some of the same radical ideas about the outside world and practiced many of the same brainwashing techniques among their congregations.

Koinonia is still operational to this very day under its newest moniker, Homestead Heritage. At the time, it consisted of many large, ill-adjusted families living together in community, on a farm on the Brazos River, mostly made up of ex-Mennonites, offshoots of United Pentecostals, and super legalistic fundamentalist Baptists. Incredible effort is put into this cult's façade of wholesome, old-time families living off the land, wholly and entirely separate from the evil practices of the worldly, wicked people who make up the citizenry of the nation outside of their fairy tale existence, where they enjoy a simple, self-sufficient lifestyle practicing pioneer/settler-style farming.

This group carefully presents themselves with artificial smiles and a meticulously crafted air of invitation to seduce their guests into believing the fabrication of a reality that does not actually exist. They are the blind, leading the blind, through various simulations that are meant to entice, manipulate, and coerce fearful, ignorant people who lack the mindset and skills to influence the real world into funding this giant cult, which consisted of 600 individuals in the early 90s, and is now 1,200 strong. Their methods allow them to feign simplicity, purity, holiness, and love while engaging in the most destructive forms of physical, mental, emotional, spiritual, and sexual abuse.

Throughout the year, the efforts of the commune are focused on the craft fair that takes place every Thanksgiving weekend. During this annual event, the gates of the commune swing wide to the public, inviting the curious in to see what amounts to a magnificent old-timey, theatrical production. What the curious public does not know is that what they see is produced by brainwashed individuals, manipulated by a religious fanatic and his select henchmen, hiding in plain sight behind the stunning artistry and sturdy craftsmanship displayed in every building, exhibit, and ware. The credibility that excellence can buy is astounding. We should never forget that beauty perceived is not always what it seems when one is not privy to the darkness that lies beneath.

Of course, I was completely ignorant to all of this as my family pulled into the cedar fence-lined pasture marked "parking" behind the Smith's fifteen-passenger van. It was impossible not to stare in curiosity as the most peculiar looking people I had ever seen welcomed us into what seemed like a step back in time. Men in round-toed boots, plaid shirts, and jeans held up with suspenders doffed straw hats and offered rides to the main attractions, in wagons. The wagons were pulled by enormous draft horses that dwarfed my previous idea of how big a horse could actually be. Women, with long hair done up in the holy hairstyle of the "bump and a bun," scurried to and fro in long, homemade dresses, more often than not with a baby on a hip, and anywhere from a couple to a dozen small children following in ascending ages and sizes.

The frenzied instrumentation of a bluegrass band echoed from one side of the fairgrounds while the smell of hand-rolled pastries and freshly butchered sausage on a stick drifted in from the other. Booths selling pottery, quilts, artisan wood working, and beeswax candles lined the edges of the fairgrounds as unsuspecting tourists milled around, completely enamored by the quality and craftsmanship of the products in their hands. The dull roar of the crowds of people and musical acts from the side stage was intermittently broken up by a voice cutting through the atmosphere over a loudspeaker, inviting the guests to demonstrations exhibiting sheep shearing, horse shoeing, and the like. If Walt Disney and Laura Ingalls Wilder had put their heads together, this strange world that surrounded me would most certainly have been the result.

After lunch, there was a brief pause in the hustle and bustle as the guests were invited to the main stage of a large tin-covered wooden structure the community members affectionately called "The Tabernacle." As my family and I took our seats on one of the long wooden benches that served as rows of seating for the masses, a few of the organization's leaders took to the mic to share with the few thousand in attendance the story of how the community had come to be.

The way those men presented their version of how they had created this "godly structure," after being called out to live a life separate from the evils of the world, seemed incredibly appealing to my parents. The discovery of a group of like-minded isolationists, who had discovered how to escape from normal society, drew in my parents like moths to a flame, and the system was ready to welcome them with open arms into the introductory level of indoctrination.

Unbeknownst to us, we had already garnered the attention of one of the men patrolling the fairgrounds, known within the organization as "watchers." During the few open days of interaction with the outside world, these men were charged with being on the lookout for large families, such as mine and the Smiths, who might end up being a "good fit" for the community. The "watcher" that moved in on my family was a man named Curtis Brown. His job was to take us on a front-row seat, behind-the-scenes tour of communal, agrarian living. Before I knew it, we were all seated on bales of hay in our own private horse-drawn wagon as we struck off down some backwoods trails while Mr. Brown filled us in on the history and function of different areas that our vehicle of 'literal horsepower' plodded past. Everything he said to us sounded like Heaven on Earth, when compared to the slum to which we were accustomed.

The scent of freshly tilled earth, the taste of fruit picked off trees with our own hands, and the sound of peace and quiet along the dirt roads that connected quaint cabins were enough to have us say, "Yes," to the invitation to join this group of six hundred isolationists for one of their smaller, homegroup-style Friday night meetings.

Friday night meetings, it was explained to us, were for those seeking God's will, who were not yet "covenant members" of the community. The "church's" Sunday morning services were reserved for the attendance of the commune's covenant members, which should have been the first red flag that something was terribly wrong. But after all, in more ways than one, this was my family's first rodeo.

I would later learn that the closed Sunday morning meetings at Homestead Heritage are structured by its leadership to beat the congregants into complete submission by the liberal use of fear tactics, guilt, and shame. In stark contrast, the Friday night meetings proved to paint an altogether different picture. Designed to keep perspective members interested, everything is carefully manipulated to continue the initial illusion that one had experienced at the craft fair. Those invited are fawned over and celebrated, given gifts, and have the opportunity to take part in different experiences on the farm.

Occasionally, however, mistakes were made, and I would catch a glimpse of the extreme control and abuse going on behind the scenes. Whether walking in on a husband twisting his wife's arm, her face grimacing with pain as he whispered menacingly how she "should submit and not speak out of turn again," or seeing the Brown's neighbor's son beaten mercilessly on the back porch of the adjacent property until his father's arm got tired of flailing the belt across his thirteen-year-old body, as I walked on by.

I would later learn from the boy that his father was moving up the ranks to become an elder, but his promotion had been halted, and he was "under discipline" for his son's misconduct—speaking back to a resident elder's first-born son. This is when I first began to understand that the cleaner a religion presents itself on the outside, the dirtier it is on the inside. I began to realize that the more a group tries to portray perfection and holiness, the darker the perversion lurking behind the scenes, which would be proven true to anyone who has followed the news on this group throughout the years.

Now, remember, all I wanted to do in life was play basketball with my friends, and wordsmith clever lyrics, which is exactly what I did every time I could sneak away from my controlling parents. But now, every Friday and Saturday, I could be

23

found pressed into service in a variety of nineteenth-century farm chores. Walking behind horses, picking up freshly-tilled sweet potatoes, or flailing a pitchfork to throw loose hay up onto an overflowing horse drawn wagon in the sweltering Texas heat, I found myself living out Weird Al Yankovic's "Amish Paradise," the popular parody of Coolio's hit, "Gangster Paradise." It was quite a culture shock.

In the first meeting we attended, our family was instructed to get rid of all electronics and any form of digital media, as such devices were "worldly," and watching TV or listening to the radio were deadly sins. Such things have no place under the roof of a "godly home." As an alternative to all worldly forms of distraction, the elders of the church made sure we were all provided with Bibles, but they gave my parents strict instruction that we children were not to read a word of it without our parents present to explain to us what they had learned from the teachings of the leadership, so as to "protect us from falling into deception."

However, in the coming months, I continued to earn my budding reputation as the "rebellious son," hiding in my room's cramped closet, thumbing through every page, and scrutinizing each verse meticulously. In a few short months, I had read the entire Bible, book by book, chapter by chapter, verse by verse. In doing so, I unknowingly developed a unique relationship with truth that served to protect my mind from the indoctrination of the cult leaders. When they or my parents would attempt to indoctrinate me with manipulative lies, I had what I can only describe as an inner voice of discernment that would tell me if what was being said was true or not.

Over the course of subsequent meetings, we were slowly introduced to all the rules. It may shock you, the reader, to know that God smiles upon straw hats and frowns upon felt, that the degree to which one's boot is pointed versus rounded off can evoke God's wrath out of no-where. And God forbid that a woman's ankles be seen, as she would surely "cause her brother to fall."

Please keep in mind that my family was still living in the hood, where the attire was dictated by the latest season's line of FUBU and Ecko. Now imagine that suddenly my mother and sisters are growing their hair out to facilitate the appropriate "bump and a bun" while donning floor scraping blue denim skirts and homemade long-sleeved shirts. I was mortified and embarrassed to even walk out my own door as my neighborhood friends began to refer to us as, "The Little House on the Prairie."

After two years of weekly travel from the ghetto of Oak Cliff to the farmland fairytale in Waco, the elders called on my parents to take the covenant member exam concerning the church's articles of faith, which, if passed, would extend the invitation to engage at the next level, culminating in a move into the commune, and access to the previously forbidden and mysterious Sunday services. My parents spent countless hours preparing for the exam, taking their frustration and anger out on us in ever increasing forms of abuse, all in an effort to make us presentable for the inspection of the leadership as a family in good standing. Finally, feeling prepared and full of confidence, they left our home for Waco to take the test, determining our future. A passing grade would bring a radical change, geographically, and a full immersion into the cult life. Their failure to pass would mean our ex-communication from the community, and our family would once again find ourselves completely absent of any community and relationship, toxic or otherwise, outside of the four walls of our rundown home.

My siblings and I sat awaiting the results of their trip with varying levels of conflicting emotions, knowing that no matter what the outcome of our parents' meeting that day, that our lives were about to shift in a big way.

CHAPTER 4
FROM BAD TO WORSE

F ail to pass, they did. The weekly trips to the farm came to a screeching halt, and we found ourselves once again, very much alone.

For a period of time, my parents tried going here and there, looking for other groups to which they could attach themselves. Each group expressed variations of the same root belief systems. All were driven by their fear, disgust and outright hatred of the world and it's "evil pleasures." The focus of each group was to make sure that one's actions lent themselves to the appeasement of an angry God in a pathetically desperate pursuit of a someday salvation; and without fail, every camp saw themselves as a "faithful remnant" separating themselves from the ever-increasing multitude of hellbent sinners living wrath-provoking lives out in the ever-darkening world.

Most explorations were short lived, including a brief stint of attachment to a group that, to this day, I jokingly refer to as the "Gothardites." Led by devout fundamentalist Bill Gothard, this group was almost religious enough to capture my parents' devotion, but not quite. At least during this time, we learned that Cabbage Patch dolls were possessed by the devil, and we were instructed to burn all the Tonka trucks that my little brothers had been playing with because their namesake was apparently the name of a Native American god. Who knows what would have happened if that evil had been allowed to stay in our house?!

I will never forget seeing the Duggar family on a popular television show years later and smelling the Gothard influence all over them at first glance. I even mentioned to my wife, "See how squeaky clean this family is presenting themselves? There's some nasty secrets going on there, and it's only a matter of time before the proof rises to the surface." It is funny how one can spot the influence of groups like these with such ease if one is familiar with their style of presentation and tailored language. The bottom line is that freedom is never found in the "protection" of religion, and those who live in its bondage will eventually manifest the hidden brokenness that it breeds.

For all our searching, however, none of these off-the-beaten-path groups of religious isolationists carried quite the appeal that the Waco community possessed. My parents, refusing to allow Heritage Homestead's diagnoses of "unfit for community" to dictate their socioreligious lives, got to work locating and reaching out to other families who had suffered the same fate of excommunication from similar religious sects.

Before I knew it, my parents had formed their own little cult under the simple name of "Home Church," becoming the self-proclaimed leaders of several others who had also been rejected by hyper-religious organizations. Born of toxicity, rejection, and abuse, this little group became more and more secluded and isolated from society every year. For us, as the children of the leader of a cult, we saw first-hand the control that goes with this type of religion.

My siblings and I quickly learned that our number one purpose in life was to make our parents and the "Home Church" look good. If we failed in this, the wrath of my parents would surely come. My parents became so consistently abusive behind closed doors that it became the new normal. I remember many times, sitting at my father's work bench with the bright light of his table-mounted work lamp pointed directly in my eyes while those in authority over me repeatedly yelled scriptures in a vain attempt to make me submit and align with whatever latest teaching or instruction had been revealed to them. When the beatings would come, I was forced to quote scriptures between strikes of the belt, one of their favorites being, "The eye that mocks a father and scorns to obey a mother will be picked out by the ravens of the valley and eaten by the vultures!" (Prov 30:17 NRSV). Of course, all of this was done for my own good so that I might not be lost to the eternal fires of hell for failing to submit to the holy standard and requirements of God.

But amid all of this, the most painful part of it had nothing to do with me. I was the youngest of the first set of five children, and my five younger siblings were still very small. I had become their protector and guide through the pain of constant beatings and controlling manipulation that took place behind the closed doors of our home. While outwardly maintaining a façade as the head of our household, my dad was, in reality, the errand boy for my controlling mother. In fact, she would beat him as frequently as he beat us. Her religious spirit called all the shots, and he just did her bidding with complete subjection.

Shortly after my fifteenth birthday, I came to the sudden realization that I was much larger than my father's five foot six frame. You may be familiar with the story of how old-time circus acts trained elephants to stay in place, tethered to a ridiculously small stake in the ground, by introducing and solidifying the concept of captivity when the elephant was a baby and incapable of escaping what would later, upon reaching their maturity, become laughable levels of constraint.

Well on this day, the imaginary rope tied to the misconception of my powerlessness snapped when my dad came at me upon my mother's command, intent on another beating for my rebellious attitude. To the surprise of both of us, I met him head on and threw him across the room with a vengeance. I will never forget the look on his face as he picked himself up off the floor; and more importantly, the realization that the beatings were over and that I finally had the upper hand, at least physically. My father could no longer use me as his punching bag at the whim of my mother. It was a small, but welcome, victory. For although the other forms of abuse continued, at least they came without the accompaniment of physical pain. Even so, there was only so much I could take, and I began to plot my escape, complete with plans to rescue my smaller siblings from the horrendous acts of violence masquerading as the will of God. I became fixated on one dream, one objective, one phrase… "getting out."

At the age of fifteen, I ran away for the first time—then another time. Each attempt at freedom from the insanity would find me right back at my front door, police in tow, handed over to the craziness that was my family. I finally found some reprieve when, at sixteen, I ran away for the final time. I snuck away in the middle of the night with a few precious belongings. An older sister, who had already pulled off the great escape at twenty-something, was waiting for me in the parking lot of the little, old-school Baptist church down the street. This time, she had connections with a social worker, and the backing of the law, as they shared a solution I was not expecting but welcomed with open arms. "Did you know now that you are sixteen, you can legally emancipate yourself from your parents?" The question was posed.

"Sign me up!" I exclaimed.

For someone who had no idea of how the real world worked, the legal steps toward emancipation were confusing—full of emotion, anger, and fear of the unknown. My case was handed over to Child Protective Services, and the following six months of my life went by in a blur. At my request, and upon my testimony of abuse, my younger siblings were removed from my parents' home and placed in a Dallas area Buckner Children's Home. I went from the home of my sister's friend to a quick stint in foster care, and finally landed in my aunt's house. She and my uncle, whom I had only seen once a year for the last several years, selflessly cared for all my needs and assumed power of attorney for me as we awaited our day in court.

Unexpectedly, during the first few days of my newfound freedom, my ability to see things in a supernatural dimension took a drastic and dark turn. Despite constant assurance from my new-found protectors that there was no way I would be sent back to my parents' house, I was filled with a constant sense of dread. Although I did not have language to articulate it clearly at the time, I understand now that I was very much under the oppression of the spirit of fear, to be more accurate, terror. My gifting went from seeing the future and supernatural dimensions with my spiritual eyes, to seeing demonic manifestations leaning into the physical dimension with my natural eyes. Everywhere I looked, I saw evil faces leering at me from behind trees and from within bushes in broad daylight. Shadowy figures stood at the foot of my bed at night, hovering menacingly and muttering in demonic tongues. It took me several days to figure out how to "turn it off" and bring the ghostly apparitions to an end. The two things I did not understand at the time were:

1. The ability to see into the spirit realm was a gift that with proper understanding and steward-ship would greatly benefit myself and others.

2. That when I turned off seeing into the system of darkness, I turned off the ability to see into the Kingdom of Light at the same time.

It would be years before that gift would be revived within the context of healthy, Kingdom, prophetic culture.

When the day in court that we had been waiting for finally came, my stomach dropped as I was hit with the news. Because of freedom of religion, and a lack of evidence in the form of image, video, or audio to reinforce the allegations of abuse, my little brothers and sisters would be sent back to the hell on Earth that awaited them in my parents' house in Oak Cliff. Such evidence was, of course, impossible to provide when any kind of camera or recorder was considered "worldly" and not allowed in the home. The trau-matic shock of this severe disappointment took my breath away as I sat in disbelief at the news. But my disappointment quickly turned to a silent rage, partnered with bitterness. I felt an authentic hatred, fueled by the accusatory voice in my head, condemning my inability to protect my younger siblings.

Being emancipated from my parents' control and excommunicated from both cults were personal wins, but those victories rang hollow next to the tormenting voice reminding me of the life to which my little brothers and sister had been sentenced.

My easygoing, fun-loving, hopeful personality died that day as I exchanged my God-given personality for a cheap, smiling, and masked exterior. All the while, an internal hatred for my parents raged in my heart. Nights were the worst; I was never at peace, and I tried my best to dull the nagging torment of the accusatory voice with daydreams of murdering my parents so that my siblings could experience the freedom that I had. I could not enjoy my freedom; I was in a state of constant misery and ignorance, and in desperate need of the freedom that can be found only within the power of forgiveness.

Thankfully, I was about to be introduced to a family that held that key for me, and who in more ways than one, would change my life forever.

The ability to see into the spirit realm was a gift that with proper understanding and stewardship would greatly benefit myself and others.

CHAPTER 5
A FRESH START

One of my older sisters had preceded me in my escape and had begun attending a small, Baptist church in the heart of the Dallas-Fort Worth metroplex. Even though I was being eaten alive from the inside out with bitterness and hatred of my parents, I found moments of peace in the calm, orderly lines of the pews, the predictability of the three hymns followed by three points, and a poem, all of which were enjoyed by the authentically kind, Jesus-loving congregants who gathered there.

The church had a history of recruiting youth pastors from the nearby independent, fundamental Baptist Bible college in a neighboring suburb and had recently hired a young couple from the Amarillo area, Mark and Cinda Urquhart.

Mark was a passionate evangelist and a real man's man. His enthusiastic communication style and authentic love for Jesus really drew me in and inspired me. The first tattoo I ever got, the Hebrew word reverend—meaning to be feared—was inspired by a message Mark preached on the seven sons of Sceva, who were ridiculed by a demon saying, "Jesus I know, and Paul I know; but who are you?" (Acts 19:15 NKJV). Mark fervently admonished us to be people who the devil knew, people who intentionally did damage to the works of darkness here on the earth. To this day, I can remember several of his Wednesday night messages, and I still love to hear him preach!

Mark's beautiful wife, Cinda, would hug me upon my arrival, and departure, each Sunday morning and Wednesday night, while saying, "I love you," with the most sincerity I had ever heard in an individual's voice. I did not have the capacity to receive that level of authentic love and would stand awkwardly not knowing what to say or do, but at the same time feeling more valued and more loved than I had ever felt in my life.

After a month or two of working my first job as a video store clerk, which was the most rebellious and worldly job I could find, considering my Amish-ish roots, I finally scraped up enough funds to purchase my first vehicle. It was a cream-colored Isuzu Pup Truck with a rusted out right, rear fender. I had to hit the starter with a crowbar to get it to start, and the first week I owned it, the back window was broken out in front of my aunt's house by someone who wanted the solitary ten-inch sub that bumped in exhaustion behind the driver's seat. It was in every sense of the word what was defined in my neighborhood as a "hooptie," and would never boast a back window again, but the freedom that it provided me was invaluable.

From the first day I had the Isuzu's keys in my possession, I spent every possible moment at the Urquhart's house, intrigued by how they interacted as a healthy, loving family. In addition, they went out of their way to make sure I knew I was a part of it, a fact that seemed too good to be true; I could not wrap my head around it.

One evening as we sat in their living room after watching a Cowboys game, Mark carefully brought up the subject of my estranged family. With all the wisdom and kindness imaginable, he posed a statement to me that I needed to hear but could not understand in the midst of my broken state, "Bro, you've got to forgive your parents because it's killing you."

From a healthy perspective, this was obviously the most loving and necessary thing that could have been said to me in that moment, but the bitterness in my heart twisted the truth that he had spoken, and all I could hear was a lie screaming in my mind, "Your parents don't deserve to be forgiven! Remember everything they have done to you! How can he be taking your parents' side in this?"

In a rage, I stood up, gave Mark a "thumbs out, middle fingers up, double barreled" salute, and stormed out of the house. I may not have been able to hear him in the moment, but for the next two weeks his words played like a loop in my mind, "You've got to forgive your parents because it's killing you." As these words of truth rang relentlessly over and over, my heart began to resonate with them, and I knew deep down that it was true.

Finally, one night I found myself driving to Mark's house, ringing the doorbell, and after being greeted with open arms, he led me through a simple prayer that would set me free and allow the authentic Dubb to begin to live again. It was a prayer of forgiveness toward my parents and an acknowledgment of trust in God to take care of my younger siblings. It was as if an eight-hundred-pound gorilla had stepped off my chest. I was free from the guilt and shame with which the enemy had tormented me, as well as the deep, sincere hatred I had held in my heart for so long.

If Mark had not been my hero before that night, he certainly was now. I wanted nothing more than to follow in his footsteps, and even my passion for all things music took a backseat to the goal of becoming a life-changing youth pastor. Although I continued my current musical pursuits (experimenting with different styles of music and forming bands with anyone who owned an instrument and claimed to know how to play) I made a decisive move and enrolled in the same small Baptist Bible college that Mark had attended.   He later transferred to Dallas Baptist University, finished his degree, and claimed his diploma.

Bible college was an interesting experience, to say the least. My unusually broad knowledge and retention of scripture, partnered with the ability to discern falsehoods masquerading as truth that I had developed while hiding in the closet of my parents' house, were both a blessing and a curse, in this new environment. I was sent to the president's office on multiple occasions for challenging my professors on denominationally influenced, ridiculous doctrinal statements that they had made to the class. In addition to these frequent run-ins, I was frustrated to find the constant reinforcement of the theology of an angry God, whose holy justice demanded punishment by murdering His own Son, to be the primary presentation of the Gospel above all else. It was a belief system that I would learn was known in theological circles as Penal Substitution Atonement Theory. This theory never settled well in my heart and resulted in my embracing Jesus while keeping Father at an arm's length. I would later discover, and be reconciled to, the Orthodox view of the atonement, Christus Victor, which would reunite me with my good, kind, and loving heavenly Father.

A couple of years later, I found myself fully disillusioned with Bible college and jumped at the chance to follow the Urquharts back to Amarillo to lead worship for the youth group of which they had assumed pastorship.

Little did I know that Amarillo—in all its flat, windy yellowness—would hold the greatest gift for my future that I would ever receive; a green eyed, curly headed, dancing beauty who would first catch my eye and then capture my heart!

CHAPTER 6
FLAT AND YELLOW

My move to Amarillo, Texas, was, in many ways, quite a shocking transition. The landscape was the most striking and obvious difference. The flat plains of tall, yellow grass stretching as far as the eye could see in every direction, stood in sharp contrast to the heavily trafficked highways and countless buildings that had blocked any view beyond a few hundred yards of what had been my usual surroundings. The wind blew with an unrelenting constancy, sweeping extreme weather down from the east side of the Rockies and across the great plains with the heated intensity of a blast furnace in the summer, and the razor-sharp chill of subzero temperatures in the winter.

I exchanged the hip-hop and cholo-influenced atmosphere that was familiar to me for a primarily white, slow country living, good ol' boy culture. And although it, too, had its pros and cons, at least the new culture meant that the probability of my getting shot or stabbed dropped significantly, and I could get used to that.

As I learned to navigate my new surroundings, I continued to follow Mark and Cinda wherever they ministered, to different youth groups in different churches, doing my best to lead the groups of students into a genuine encounter with Jesus and prepare their hearts to be able to receive the powerful, anointed words that Mark spoke from his heart every time he had the microphone.

Shortly after arriving in the Texas panhandle, I found myself leading worship for Mark's youth group in a small-town church thirty miles northeast of Amarillo. This was my first exposure to a healthy church outside of the Baptist denomination, and I enjoyed the laid back format of the non-denominational, seeker-friendly environment. I found myself intrigued by the light, charismatic culture that was slowly beginning to develop in the church.

Since my arrival from Dallas, Mark had begun to share testimonies with me about his encounters with the Holy Spirit. The most interesting story was of one afternoon when he was lying on the carpet behind his desk in his office, and he had cried out to God saying, "If You have anything else for me, I have got to have it!" In that moment, he had experienced what he called the baptism of the Holy Spirit; words that he did not understand had begun to flow from his lips, something he called speaking in tongues.

One night, after leading worship where Mark had passionately preached to the few hundred youth that crowded the main sanctuary of the church, a longing in my own heart drew my mind back to Mark's story. I desired to know more of the power and presence of God than just the intentional friendship with Jesus that I had been cultivating. Although I still did not know what it was that I was asking for in the moment, and certainly had no idea what I would experience over the next few weeks, I closed my eyes and uttered a prayer reminiscent of my first conversation with God at six years old, "Holy Spirit, if the baptism of You is real... I want it."

I wish I had a cool story of feeling supernatural fire manifesting above my head and falling from the heavens upon me, but instead, I felt absolutely nothing. I shrugged my shoulders and reengaged with Mark's message. However, over the next few weeks, I began to experience an unfamiliar phenomenon. It was as if the prayer for wisdom that I had prayed since age eleven, and the relationship with truth that I had developed in the closet of my parents' house, had suddenly come to life. I began to supernaturally know things that were going on, to inexplicably understand why these things were happening, and most importantly, know what should be done in the moment to shift the current reality to where it should be. Although I did not have the language at the time, my relationship with what I now call the "trinity" of truth— knowledge, understanding, and wisdom—had been activated in my life from this invited infilling of the Holy Spirit, and my life would never be the same. Additionally, sight into the spirit realms that I had worked so hard to turn off in terror at age sixteen began to open back up, but this time without the sinister throngs of demonic characters pressing their way in upon me to arrest my attention and paralyze my progress.

A few Wednesday nights later, I found myself sitting in the same row, in the same setting; but instead of listening to Mark, I was pondering my newfound "superpowers." I finally concluded that this could only be the result of my invitation of the baptism of the Holy Spirit into my life, and since I now had evidence that this experience was real, it only stood to reason that the gift of tongues must be real as well. Upon that realization, I whispered a more confident prayer of invitation, "Holy Spirit, I want my prayer language, please give me the gift of tongues." I sat there waiting for a supernatural flow of heavenly language to burst forth from my lips in the same way that Mark had described. And again, nothing.

But wait, an odd, two syllable word that I had never heard before hit my mind. I brushed it off, still looking for a replication of Mark's story to manifest. But here the word came again, and again. Not knowing what else to do, I quietly spoke the word that I had heard, and to my surprise, another unknown word immediately hit my mind.

Obediently, I uttered it and was rewarded with hearing a short phrase. From there a small set of words and phrases flowed from my mouth, and although I still did not understand exactly what was going on, I knew that what I was experiencing had value and carried weight on some yet undefinable level. From that day on, the activation of this gift became a part of my daily devotional routine as I trusted with faith that my spirit was, at the very least, agreeing with what God wanted in and through my life.

Whether I was putting into practice my newfound gift of heavenly tongues while enjoying the latest Charlie Hall CD or rattling off a freshly penned sixteen bars over a simple (Roland TR-) 808 beat, one thing was for certain, I was always running my mouth. As consistently as one could find me leading worship somewhere on Wednesday nights, on the weekends, one could find me with a mic in my hand pursuing my rockstar dream.

I had hit the ground running in the Texas Panhandle, looking for musicians with whom to form a band. Although I explored wildly varied genres in my musical endeavors, it always came back to hip-hop for me. My love for the lyrical prowess of true MCs had expanded to include a short-lived but wildly popular genre of the time known as "rap-core," a showcase of lyrical skill, set to driving metal riffs. My black CD binder of DMX and Nas albums, carefully encased in plastic sleeves with the cover art inserted behind each one, expanded to include artists like Papa Roach, Limp Bizkit, and my new favorite band, P.O.D.

Aside from genuinely enjoying P.O.D.'s San Diego homegrown sound, I was fascinated by the fact that even though they were overt in their passion for Jesus, they were constantly on tours with artists like Marilyn Manson, Korn and Slipknot. There just seemed to be something so right about a group who was unapologetically in love with Jesus, and yet whose craftsmanship warranted the approval of mainstream society. It was and is remarkable that this approval came in a time when 90% of Christian music either sucked or came off as blatant counterfeit copies of what was popular in current mainstream culture. I had always had the thought in the back of my mind that if we were made in the image of the Master Creator of all things, that we should be the ones expressing the best of all things creative.

To be honest though, my favorite thing about P.O.D. was how they were so unfazed by the backlash of the watchful pharisees who would write articles expressing their righteous indignation concerning a band that had the audacity to claim to be comprised of Christ followers, and yet played festivals with musical acts who claimed to be Satanists and went on tours sponsored by Bud Light.

It still makes me laugh today. Those rants simply revealed their ignorance concerning the important truths, that if we are the light of the world, we are called to show up in the darkness. If we are the salt of the earth, then the places without flavor, or worse, are in decay, are in desperate need of exactly the preservation that we carry. Little did I know that in the future I would become a target for these same types of "holier than thou" pundits of religion for taking a similar stance of infiltration upon a very different stage.

Not long after my arrival in Amarillo, I had pulled together a group of talented musicians, and after hours of practice and countless song writing sessions, we began to work the Christian music scene in Amarillo and the surrounding area, experiencing modest levels of grass root success. My side project was a straight up rap duo in which I partnered with a local artist and talented producer.

Music was my passion, my life, and I was fixated on it being my destiny. I would drive anywhere, anytime, to perform for anybody. I slowly built enough of a reputation that I got to open for many of the bigger name Christian bands and rap acts at various music venues and festivals all over Texas, and the surrounding states. However, seeing my band's name etched in the bright lights of the marquee in the headliner spot continued to be the elusive dream for the next ten years of my life. I was always almost good enough… but not quite. It was a mirror of the belief system that I subconsciously held at my core, one that had been beaten into my performance-based mentality by my parents' unattainable and warped standards.

But, as I have come to learn, our current passion may not hold the fullness of our purpose and destiny within it, but if we are wise enough to follow it, we will be led toward what that passion holds for our God-created purpose.

One day, a friend of mine who served as a resident assistant in Cross Hall at West Texas A&M asked me to come by and rap at a dance she was putting on as a program for her residents. I was not one to turn down a gig, so of course I said yes. That night, while standing on a little stage, dropping some freshly wordsmithed lyrics, a beautiful girl with long curly hair, dancing in the crowd to the sound of the beat caught my eye. I made a mental note that as soon as the performance was over, I was going to go and "holler at her."

After finishing the song, I began to make my way through the crowd of lively college students milling around, trying to decide where they should head next. Eventually, I caught a glimpse of the curly hair through a break in the crowd and walked up behind a casual conversation the girl was having with her friend. I understood the strongest lead in my game was humor, and sure enough, a pause in their dialogue offered the perfect opportunity for a witty comment in reference to the topic of their conversation. The girl laughed and turned to see who was injecting himself into her one-on-one conversation. I extended my hand and smiled in my usual, friendly, easygoing manner, "My name is Dubb, what's yours?"

"Beth," she smiled back as I found myself caught off guard by the prettiest hazel eyes I had ever seen. I thought to myself, "This girl is way out of my league… but I'm going to give this my best shot!"

The next thirty minutes flew by and were spent in easy, introductory conversation, intentionally peppered with my trademark humor, which was met, thankfully, by Beth's contagious laugh and captivating smile, and not so fortunately by the defensive glare of Beth's friend. Eventually, we realized that the common room had emptied, but I was not ready for the night to end. I extended an invite for her and her friend to go back to my place to watch a movie and hang out; my invitation was met with enthusiasm from Beth and begrudging agreement from her friend.

This night would mark the beginning of an awesome friendship, one that we both desired to grow into something more. However, there was one thing that stood in the way of our taking the relationship to the next level. It was the one non-negotiable requirement that I had for anyone that I would date, but I had a plan.

CHAPTER 7
NEVER ASK ME AGAIN

The one non-negotiable standard when it came to my dating life was that the girl would have a relationship with Jesus. It broke my heart to find out that because of some cruel interactions and religious judgment that she had experienced as a kid from some so-called "Christians," Beth wanted nothing to do with church, Christians, or their Jesus.

I cannot say that I blamed her. In the words of Bishop T.D. Jakes, "The best people I have ever met were Christians… and the worst people I have ever met have been Christians." Although quite a sad statement, I, too, have found this to be true in my life and could easily understand where Beth was coming from.

However, I also had an ace my pocket—an extremely likable and fiery evangelist who just happened to offer an opportunity for people to meet Jesus every time he preached. I knew that if I could get Beth in a room with Mark just one time, it would be game over. So, every Wednesday, and I mean every Wednesday, I asked her to go hear me play at Mark's youth group, and every Wednesday I received the same response, "Um, no thanks." Delayed but not discouraged, I settled in for the long haul. I knew that one day that answer would change, and that one shot was all I needed.

Although it was evident that we liked each other, I had to play it cool and keep the relationship in the "friend zone." Afraid that I would simply reenforce her firmly established perception of judgmental Christians who looked down on her, I felt like I could not tell her that I could not date anyone who was not a Christian. And I could tell she was puzzled by my lack of commitment to a relational title when we were hanging out every day.

So, we hung out. Beth came to my rock shows every weekend, and every weeknight we watched movies, listened to music, or I watched her play "Dance, Dance Revolution" with her friends in her dorm's third floor common area. This went on for several weeks, until I finally got a different response to my usual Wednesday night question. "If I go one time, will you never ask me again?" Beth asked, rolling her eyes. "

You got it," I calmly replied, but on the inside, I could barely contain my excitement. "You are done for," I whispered under my breath as I turned to walk up the stairs of my apartment to retrieve my Breedlove guitar.

And done for she was! Cinda Urquhart greeted Beth at the door with her classic hug. Mark delivered a passionate message about the love of Jesus with the authenticity and inspiration only he could generate. And guess what? Sure enough, like clockwork, the invitation to anyone who would like to get to know this Jesus personally was extended. And... Beth headed down the aisle!

I could not have been more excited. Mark prayed with her, and it was a wrap! With the one non-negotiable out of the picture, I asked Beth to be my girlfriend on the way back to her dorm that night. That night was the beginning of eight months of dating, which ended with a proposal accompanied by a $25 ring.

Beth and I got married at ages twenty and twenty-one. I wore my classic west coast style Dickies, blue jeans, and K-Swiss white on whites. Beth wore a beautiful red and black, flowered dress. It was a small event, attended by a few close friends. Mark officiated, and answered his phone in the middle of the ceremony. We were young, dumb, and very much in love. Thank goodness for love, because things got very hard, very fast.

Beth's decision to marry and remain with me in the Texas Panhandle, against some of her family's wishes, came with several financial repercussions. Looking back, I can see how the rockstar-dream chasing, white rapper having distracted their gifted, dancer-college-student daughter away from a promising career in dance would cause any parent concern. But unfortunately, at that time I did not have the relational skills to navigate the two very different worlds, values, or languages.

In addition to that, I lost my job three days after our wedding, then my car broke down. And as if to add insult to injury, I promptly pulled a muscle in my back so severely that I had to pop ibuprofen like M&Ms just to get through the day. For richer and poorer, in sickness and in health became very real in short order, but Beth was amazing through it all. There were many nights that we dug through the couch cushions, looking for change to make a big night out of McDonald's fifty-cent sundaes. Or I would pawn my guitar so we could get gas and some frozen burritos from Walmart. This earned Beth the nickname of, "My Burrito or Bentley Girl." I have yet to meet a woman who can be so content with so little, and yet also enjoy the finer things in life, with class, and walk comfortably among the wealthy and influential when an opportunity presents itself.

However, at that time we were far from our first experience with the finer things in life. I was never one to be without a job, so the day after losing my job, I took two others. One was as a night clerk at the local Allsup's gas station, a thankless job that consisted mainly of frying burritos and chimi-changas for the seemingly endless line of ham-mered college students that had stumbled out of the local honkey-tonk and streamed through the doors all night. The second job was as a bus driver for the local school district, transporting groups of boisterous students back and forth from outlying residences, on dirt roads, to the brick school-houses in the middle of town. I would work 10:00 p.m. to 6:00 a.m. at the gas station, drive the bus for the morning run, sleep for a few hours, and be back at the bus barn for the afternoon run.

I knew this was not the life for me, and I was also growing increasingly discouraged in my pur-suit of a record deal. Slowly but surely, I began to let go of that dream and move the rap and rock portion of my life toward the hobby side, while taking the worship-leading side of my music obsession more seriously. This decision paid off, and I finally accepted my first full-time position as the worship leader at a local church.

This began a nominally successful ten-year career in the American church. I wore too many different hats in too many different churches to mention here. I became fluent in the seeker friendly, light charismatic, nondenominational world and discovered that I could add value in many different areas.

Livable success felt pretty good to the boy who had grown up in poverty, and then lived on the meager money to be made via part-time jobs, balanced with the feast or famine reality of the music scene. So, with a new level of comfortability, my dreams slowly shrank until the highest possibility in my mind for impacting the world became that of being the worship leader of a large church. Deep down, I knew I was made for more, and quite frankly, that I was bigger than the four walls of a church. But with consistent effort, I was eventually able to ignore that nagging voice, and I half-heartedly convinced myself that what I was experiencing was the best that this life had to offer me.

This worked for several years, until the summer before I would turn thirty, when another voice popped up in my heart, asking the same question every single day, "What is The Kingdom?"

"What is The Kingdom?"

"What is The Kingdom?"

I heard this question every morning when I woke up. By now, my meager growth in the prophetic enabled me to know that it was the Holy Spirit asking the question, but that did not help matters much because I did not know the answer. So, I began asking everyone I knew the same question. Most often I was met with a puzzled look and offered some weak sauce answer like, "Well… it's Heaven," "It's the church," or "It's the family of God." Although I knew that all three of these things were components of, or at least held attributes of The Kingdom, I knew even more strongly that the answer I was looking for had not yet been found.

Two months later, with the question still ringing in my ears, I found myself taking a group of youth ministry students to a conference in Colorado Springs. After sitting through a particularly "inspiring" service, in which the speaker had gone to great lengths to point out how the whole world was going to hell in a hand basket and the students in the room better get their friends saved immediately, due to Jesus' imminent return, I sat outside and leaned up against the wall of the church. As the students ate pizza and played football, I was having a serious internal discussion with Jesus.

"Jesus, either You are as powerful as I think that You are… and Your Holy Spirit really lives inside of me… which means I have the ability to change the world… or You are an impotent God and everything that this joker just said is true… the darkness is getting greater and greater, the world is going to hell in a hand-basket, and our only hope is for You to come back on a rescue mission before things get too bad."

Holy Spirit's response to my query was both familiar and frustrating, "What is The Kingdom?"

I barely had time to roll my eyes before my phone rang, and to my surprise, I saw the number of a friend of mine from New Mexico on the screen. After initial greetings, his next words could not have carried a greater clarion call of destiny, "Hey man, we are having a little conference down here. Got a couple of folks coming in from up north to talk about The Kingdom. I think you should come." Of course, I accepted his invitation.

A few months later, I found myself and a few friends making the six hour drive to a tiny town in southern New Mexico, where I would hear the message of The Kingdom for the first time in my life, and more importantly, be given the gift of a book by Dr. Myles Munroe entitled, *Rediscovering the Kingdom*.

Even though I struggle to read, and it is my last choice for a learning medium, I could not put this book down. I read it multiple times in a row, and for the first time, I found a definition of The Kingdom that settled the question in my heart satisfactorily as I read Dr. Munroe's eloquent statement, "God's original purpose and intent was to rule that which is seen, (the visible world), through that which is unseen, (the invisible world). He would do this through the unseen, (the Spirit of God in man), living in the unseen (spirit of man), and living in the seen, (the physical body), on the scene, (the earth).[1] Or, more simply put, "The Kingdom is the extension of the heart and the authority of God from Heaven on Earth through you." To this day, after the scriptures, no book has impacted me or shaped my life more deeply than this work of Myles'.

---

[1] (Munroe 2013)

All of a sudden, everything began to make sense. I now understood why James Smith's invitation to an eternal, fluffy cloud, and harp-filled existence had held no appeal for me. If I was made for Heaven, my name would be angel. But my name was Dubb, and I was made for here! The earth was the very place that God intended me to fulfill my purpose and destiny of being His representative in this physical realm. I realized for the first time that Jesus had repositioned me as a king on the earth in accordance with Revelation 1:4-6 (NKJV), and that kings have responsibility, authority, power, and the ability to determine the outcome of things around them.

I now read Jesus' title, "King of kings," in a whole new light! If He is the King of kings, and He is my king, then that indeed makes me a king! And what a humbling example of kingship Jesus had laid out before me. Although His title was King of kings, and not Servant of servants, He unequivocally out-served everybody in history and for all time. I realized that kingship in The Kingdom looked like me, developing my skillsets to be able to out-serve everybody else in the room.

I would read, meditate, catch something new, and then excitedly rush to share with Beth the ancient truths which were so new to me. "Babe! If Jesus is the King of kings and He is your King, what does that make you!?" "Well, a king I suppose," she responded, a little puzzled by my evident enthusiasm. In fact, I could not even bring myself to sit down as I excitedly paced back and forth in our tiny living room while she sat on our little denim-covered love seat.

"YES! So would you rather be served by a butler or a king?" I posed as the next question. "Well... a king," Beth stated, after a brief con-templative pause. "EXACTLY!" I almost shouted. "A butler can only serve you with what you already possess, but a king comes with his or her own authority, power, resources, favor, wealth and op-portunities, and then chooses to leverage those things on your behalf in order to take you to the next level!"

It was a funny statement coming from a young man with little authority, lacking the knowledge of how to practically leverage the power within him, and with little to no resources, favor, wealth, or opportunities to take advantage of for himself, much less leverage on behalf of others.

Beth nodded and smiled. She was obviously as amused by my overwhelming passion on the subject as she was impressed by my newfound "Heavy Revvy," (a term I had coined for deep revelation of ancient truths).

Growing more serious, I continued, "Beth, the Creator of the universe lives inside us. We should be the most valuable players at any table we are invited to. We are one with the One Who knows all the things! The answers for all of the world's problems are inside us, and we can access them because we have access to the mind of Jesus!" I paraphrased 1 Corinthians 2:16.

"Look at this!" I sat down beside her on the love seat and commenced to flip back and forth between Mark 16 and Matthew 28, in my ridiculously huge, leatherbound, comparative study Bible. "The great commission in Mark is evangelistic in nature, a clear charge to share the Gospel of Salvation with every "Living Creature," but the portion of the great commission contained in Matthew is about the Gospel of The Kingdom— teaching and training nations to do things God's way! Not show up, voice our disagreement, and then bow out, knowing that the world is going to get worse and worse!"

"I suppose that's true," Beth agreed, upon reading the passages for herself.

"Babe," I leaned back in the love seat as years of fear, helplessness, urgency, and purposelessness slipped off my shoulders, "only a cruel God would charge His children with doing something that they are not capable of accomplishing. That would doom them to an existence of failure, disappointment, and shame."

I paused for a moment as the truth settled even more deeply in my heart. Beth looked at me expectantly, "Go on...."

I looked back into her eyes with an excitement that I now get to see come alive in others when I share these truths with them. "I don't think Jesus is coming back for a while. We've got work to do! We've been praying that God would either do something or come back on a rescue mission..." I paused, searching for the right words to convey what I was just now perceiving. "But what if God already has done something by sending us as the answer to the world's needs just like Jesus came as the answer to our needs... and what if He's not coming back on a rescue mission but rather for a celebration, a wedding, when the bride has done what she has been commissioned to do?"

It was that day that my perception of my purpose in life, which up until that time had been a "try not to sin and tell as many people as I could about Jesus until I died" mentality, matured into the truth that I was here on Earth to represent the heart and authority of my Father. I was to bring solutions to the issues of the world so that people might experience the goodness of God here on Earth, not just when they died and went to Heaven. If it is indeed the goodness of God that leads men to repentance (Romans 2:4), what better way to lead people into a relationship with Him than to introduce them to His goodness by showing them how He is the answer to every problem, temporal as well as eternal?

CHAPTER 8
ORIGINAL INTENT

One truth that fully captured my heart was the understanding of the original intent of man. I would read the first chapter of Genesis over and over but was especially captured by verse 26. I had to pick up the phone and call Beau, a spiritual son who had grown into a peer and theological sounding board over the years, to talk it out. "Bro, philosophers have been trying to figure out the reason man exists and the purpose for which he exists for thousands of years, and the answer has been sitting here in Genesis 1:26 the whole time!"

"Okay?" Beau responded, obviously intrigued but unsure of where I was headed with the conversation.

"Hear me out," I continued. "There is a difference between the reason for which something exists and the purpose for which it exists. Take the lightbulb, for example. The reason it exists is because an inventor had the idea and the wherewithal to manifest his creation from the unseen realm of the imagination into the seen realm of physical reality. But the purpose of the lightbulb is to shed light! So, you can have a lightbulb in its carton, on the shelf, in the closet with the door closed—it has a reason for existing but is altogether out of purpose! And so, it is with most of humanity!"

"Go on… what does the verse say?" Beau queried.

"Wait for it!" I continued excitedly. "Let me set the scene: we are eavesdropping on a conversation amongst The Trinity, Who has existed eternally within the context of loving relationship. They enjoy this reality so much that They decide to expand the family by creating sons and daughters! Listen…" I began to read Genesis 1:26 (NKJV) from the Bible that lay open on my desk in front of me, "Then God said, 'Let Us make man in Our image, according to Our likeness;'" I paused. "That right there is the reason we exist! If we are made in His likeness and image, and He is and looks like loving relationship, then that is the reason that we exist! To experience the love of God, love Him back, and live forever in a reciprocal love relationship!"

"I'm with you, go on!" Even over the phone I could tell Beau was tracking with me, and his excitement level was beginning to rise to match mine.

I continued to read the verse, repeating the first portion now that it would be heard within the proposed context. "Then God said, 'Let Us make man in Our image, according to Our likeness…,'" I paused for effect before continuing, "'…and let them have dominion.'" I finished triumphantly.

"The reason we exist is to experience the love of God, to love Him back, and live forever within the context of loving relationship. But the purpose for which we exist is to have dominion! Not over people, but over territory, atmospheres, and things! Everyone we know has a reason for existing, but how many of them are walking in their purpose?" I finished excitedly.

"Because they don't know… no one?" Beau responded thoughtfully.

"Exactly!" I confirmed enthusiastically. "But now we know! And we gotta tell everyone!"

"But what does all this look like, practically?" Ever a voice of reason, that was Beau's next question. I laughed and leaned back in my chair, agreeing with the validity of the question, and recognizing the extreme importance of being able to communicate an effective answer as the next step for this mind-blowing revelation—to make an actual difference in the world that we lived in.

From Dr. Myles, I was introduced to Lance Wallnau. Although Lance has become a somewhat controversial figure due to his increasing involvement in politics over the last few years, I still see him as one of the greatest Kingdom Revelators of all time. To myself, I jokingly dubbed him "The Mad Scientist of The Kingdom" as I watched and rewatched his YouTube videos. He scribbled wildly on a whiteboard while describing how we should be showing up in culture as "Ninja Sheep." We were to be like Daniel and Joseph, walking with the "evil" kings of the earth, making Heaven's strategies available in practical ways so the people of this world that God loves so much could experience His goodness.

I knew that I was made for this! Time and time again, I poured over one lesson in particular; in fact, my notes were practically a full-blown transcription of his ninety-minute video on a strategy that he referred to as "The Seven Mountains."

"Listen," I eagerly began describing the concept to Tim, a trusted friend who was as intrigued by The Kingdom revelation as I was, "in every fully developed nation there are seven spheres, (or mountains to use Lance's analogy), of influence. They are religion, family, education, government, media, arts and entertainment, and business." Tim nodded, indicating that he was with me so far. I continued, "The people with the most influence or authority at the tops of those mountains call the shots that shape the culture of that nation, dictating the reality that the citizenry of that nation experience."

"Makes sense," Tim responded, ever the encouraging listener.

"Look back at the 70s and 80s with all of the garbage contained in books of that era like, *The Late Great Planet Earth* and *88 Reasons Jesus Is Coming Back In 1988*. I earnestly continued, "We convinced all of the sincere believers who held positions of influence and authority in our nation, whether Fortune 500 CEOs, professors at Ivy League universities, congressmen, senators, etc., that what they were doing really had no value, and if they wanted their lives to really make a difference, they would quit their 'worldly' jobs, sell everything that they owned, and hit the streets telling people about Jesus."

Tim immediately picked up on what I was saying. "What a tragedy!" he responded, already beginning to see the next few steps down my line of reasoning. "The people who knew God and carried His values and the ability to hear His voice clearly are the very people who should have stayed in those positions!"

"Exactly!" I jumped back in, "But we told them what they brought to the table had no value. Whoa!" I leaned back in my chair as a memory came flooding back to my mind. "Bro, I remember one time at youth camp when I was sixteen; closing night, they asked for everyone who had accepted Jesus that week to stand. They stood, and everybody clapped and cheered."

"And?" Tim was clearly puzzled as to the story's bearing on the current conversation.

"Next, they asked for everyone who had 'accepted the call and surrendered to the ministry' to stand."

"And you stood up?" Tim prompted.

"Yeah man, because I wanted to be a youth pastor like Mark."

"Where are you going with this?" Tim asked with a little laugh.

"Well, I stood up with a few others and some half-hearted applause started," I could remember the moment clear as day, "and as I looked down the row where I had been sitting, I could see my friends who wanted to be teachers, nurses, coaches and what not. And they all had the same look of disappointment on their faces. They were not disappointed with me; they were disappointed with themselves. It was like I could hear them saying to themselves, "If I really loved God, I would be like Dubb and go work for God in the church."

"Ahh." Understanding, Tim leaned forward. "But the work they wanted to do, if done as God's representatives and in His way, could bring just as much value to society as what you wanted to do." I nodded, affirming his observation.

"What did you do?" Tim asked.

"I sat down," I answered. "I didn't have language for it. I just knew it wasn't right. In fact," I continued as more revelation came, "I experienced the same thing in Bible college. Those of us in the youth pastor track would look at those enrolled in the missionary track and have the same type of conversation. We believed in our hearts that if we really loved God, we would go live in a mud hut in Africa, not take some cushy youth pastor job here in the states."

"Comparison is the thief of joy," Tim observed.

"Not only that," I responded, "comparison is the thief of purpose."

It was in that conversation that the necessity of affirming the value of God's call to positions in all spheres of society within the hearts of His sons and daughters became a priority in my life. Indeed, all of the church is in The Kingdom, but not all of The Kingdom is in the church. And the sooner that the body of Christ realized this truth, the better off the whole world would be for it.

I barely slept that night as nuances and aspects of these truths rose to the surface, and I gained more clarity and language around the concepts that Tim and I had discussed. I became increasingly convinced that the issues we were dealing with in society were much less a spiritual battle (indeed if it was a spiritual battle, our God would be making a pretty poor showing) and much more a matter of dealing with the consequences of decades of the sons and daughters of God not taking their rightful places in society, as architects responsible for producing heavenly culture here on Earth.

The next day would be one of the most important days of my life, as I would unknowingly agree with God's original design for my life while listening to a shorter, audio teaching of Lance's, in which he encouraged the listeners to pause the recording and putting aside false humility and insecurity, to tell God what we really wanted, what was in our hearts to do.

Right there in my little office, in a little church, in a little town in Texas, I paused the recording, took a deep breath, and spoke plainly and authentically to the Lord, "Jesus, I want to take this message of The Kingdom and the strategy of the seven mountains and share it with the leaders of culture. I want to share it with Fortune 500 CEOs, rockstars, presidents, Ivy League professors... with whomever You will open the door for me to sit and talk."

Little did I know that over the next ten years I would find myself doing exactly that, and even less did I realize the amount of process and heat that I would take along the way to get to that point. On that day I spoke as a willing son, but my training in kingship had just begun.

"The reason we exist is to experience the love of God, to love Him back, and live forever within the context of loving relationship. But the purpose for which we exist is to have dominion!

CHAPTER 9
THE HERESY HUNTERS

I t was as if the very minute I agreed with my purpose and destiny and began to engage the process to be able to walk it out into its fullness, the detractors of my mission came out of the woodwork.

And sadly, the attacks came not from unbelievers; indeed, I would come to find that the good news of The Kingdom is offensive to the religious while attractive to those who stand outside of its benefits.

The accusations came flooding in.

"Dubb's preaching a different Gospel."

"Dubb doesn't believe in going to Heaven."

"Dubb wants to take over the world."

The list went on and on.

At first, I tried to reason with these people that I would eventually, affectionately, or at least humorously, give the title of "Heresy Hunters." It sounds like a reality show, doesn't it? "Don't miss 'Heresy Hunters' tonight on A&E, 8:00 p.m. Central."

Humorous in concept, yes, but less fun when one's actual reality began to consist of countless conversations with acquaintances, or even those who I had considered friends, who would approach me with a "check in their spirit," or concern over the "heretical deception" into which I had fallen.

Life began to feel like Bill Murray's *Groundhog Day* experience, finding myself endlessly explaining that, although I still very much believed in the Gospel of Salvation, and without question recognized its ultimate importance of being the vehicle by which people entered The Kingdom, that I had also come to the realization that it was just the door into the fullness of The Gospel of The Kingdom! It was a part, but not by any means the wholeness of The Good News.

"Jesus actually never once publicly preached salvation," I pointed out. "He cited the necessity of a born again experience once in private to Nicodemus, and yet daily preached the Gospel of The

Kingdom! We have fallen short of people being able to experience the fullness of the goodness of God by preaching a Gospel about Jesus but failing to preach the very Gospel that Jesus Himself preached!"

However, the majority of the time, my scripturally backed points fell upon deaf ears, and the conversations closed with what became the all-too-common retort of, "I'll be praying for you." Which really ended up meaning that they were heading out the door to warn others, armed with the new level of clarity they had gained in our conversation surrounding my particular brand of deceptive heresy.

I found comfort during these discouraging times in seeing the same attacks launched toward not only Myles Munroe and Lance Wallnau, but also the newest additions to my library of Kingdom influence, Kris Vallotton, and Bill Johnson, from Bethel Church in Redding, California. I suppose misery loves company in all forms and fashions. Even though my stage for influence was quite insignificant compared to these giants of the faith, at least I could count myself among good company.

The "Dubb doesn't believe in going to Heaven" accusation always made me laugh. I was by no means against anyone going there if they died before Jesus came back, but I had gained the understanding that getting to Heaven was not the goal; rather, seeing Heaven come to Earth was the ultimate win! Indeed, if my attackers would simply read Revelation 21-22, it should have been clear that we get kicked out of Heaven in the end anyway! We will find ourselves walking as kings on the new Earth, God will come down out of Heaven to walk once again with man in a physical (albeit, upgraded), dimension, reminiscent of the original design of the garden reality found in Genesis 1-2, which God Himself described as "very good."

Ninety-nine percent of the time, my friendly attempts at clarification and patient direction toward the back of the book fell upon deaf ears, and it never ceased to amaze me how people would fight to hold onto their illusionary, cloud-filled, harp-strumming, utopian dream as their perception of our highest, ultimate destiny.

The charge of wanting to "take over the world" continued to be leveraged against me, regardless of how many times I would reiterate that my heart's desire was to change the world, not take it over. And that I believed this change would come by serving mankind so well that all of humanity could not help but have an encounter with the goodness of God and begin to agree with His way of doing things. Even today, there are some in what I would consider to be the same stream as myself on several levels who will still shake their heads at the "dominionistic" views that I apparently hold. To which I laugh a little and ask, "Have you ever read Genesis 1:26? It's kind of the whole point." Of course, I understand that these well-meaning folks have simply been hurt or manipulated by authority in the past. Having no model of what a healthy authority that serves and promotes (rather than controls and manipulates) looks like, makes it hard for one to grasp the concept of how radically different dominion and kingship are expressed in The Kingdom.

As if the theology of The Kingdom was not a big enough target for the Heresy Hunters, on the heels of that came the revelation of righteousness! They really hated that. You see, even after capturing the revelation of The Kingdom, I continued to struggle along for a while because the enemy constantly disqualified me in my mind from being a part of this treasure that I had discovered. "Sure, The Kingdom exists," he argued, "but its benefits are for holy people... people like Bill Johnson. Remember what you did last week? Sinners like you don't get to enjoy the benefits of The Kingdom."

I lived a conflicted existence for a period of time, torn between my excitement over the discovery of The Kingdom and the constant barrage of guilt, shame, and self-condemnation. But I faithfully continued to read Matthew 6:33 daily, and one day it finally dawned on me that Jesus specifically said to seek HIS righteousness and not my own. The minute that revelation hit my mind, I began to see righteousness and many scriptures in a whole new light!

The righteousness and benefits available for me to enjoy were found in His righteousness, not my own! My own righteousness was self-righteousness, and that did not do anybody any good! Jesus' very own righteousness was being extended to me as a gift as 2 Corinthians 5:21 stated, "He made Him who knew no sin to be sin for us, that we might become the righteousness of God in Him." (NKJV)

I knew that when I received Jesus as my Savior, I was baptized by the blood into Him (Galatians 3:27). If I was already in Him, then I must already qualify as a candidate to embody His righteousness as well, not when I die and go to Heaven, as I had been taught, but here and now.

This revelation was further confirmed by 1 John 4:17b which clearly states that, "…as He is, so are we in this world." (NKJV) Did you catch that? We are as He, Jesus, is here in this world! I could not get enough of the goodness of the true Gospel of the finished work of Christ, and the blessed ramifications of what it meant to me here and now on the earth in my current reality!

I finally understood that The Kingdom was where I belonged, and His righteousness was why I belonged.

But the good news did not stop there. My beautiful daughter, Cinda (named after Cinda Urquhart, who informed me after expressing her delight upon having a namesake, that she, herself, would be known only as "Original Cinda," and by no means was ever to be referred to as "Big Cinda") had been born the same year that I captured the revelation of The Kingdom. As my love for her grew, my disdain for Penal Substitution Atonement Theory continued to grow as well. I would sometimes stare into Little Cinda's tiny, smiling face, looking deeply into her bright, loving, trusting eyes, and try not to think of what it must have been like for Father to require the torture and death of His perfect Son, just so that He could bear the presence of sinners.

I do not know if I somehow thought that Father was unaware of these conversations I was having with myself or what, but one day He interrupted me with a question that stopped me in my tracks. "Hey Dubb," He asked gently, "would you allow me to re-introduce Myself to you?"

"Um, of course?" I stammered. I mean, what else does one say to the Creator of the Universe?

He continued, "You think that Jesus came to save you from Me." It took me a little less time to respond to this statement. "I do think that… that's all I've ever been taught."

He did not say anything else, but I knew enough from my recent, "What is The Kingdom?" journey that I had taken with Holy Spirit that this was an invitation to go on a treasure hunt, resulting in glorious revelation. Sure enough, I soon discovered the relatively recent (historically speaking) heretical roots of Penal Substitution Atonement Theory and pushed past them to discover the Orthodox belief surrounding the atonement held to by the early church fathers—a truth known today as Christus Victor.

I wept tears of joy as I discovered the truth that Father was not outside of Jesus on the cross, raining His wrath and punishment for sin upon the Son so that He could stand us, but rather in accordance with 2 Corinthians 5:19, He "was in

Christ, reconciling the world to Himself." (NKJV) Indeed, the co-existent nature of the Trinity demands unanimous agreement and presence in all things. For in Christ lives all the fullness of God in a human form (Colossians 2:9 {NLT}).

With each new level of revelation concerning the gloriousness of the true Gospel and the goodness of my Father, the witch hunt from the religious of my community intensified. After a period of time, I found myself having to work to keep bitterness from setting in against the church, based upon the constant barrage of attack from those who attended local bodies in the area, and yet, always seemed to have a rock in their hand when an opportunity came to take a shot at me.

Thankfully, after a year or two, God set me free from engaging in these fruitless conversations by simply speaking the words, "Feed only the hungry," to my heart. From that point on, I began to share the things concerning The Kingdom with people who were looking only to become rather than to debate, and I cannot tell you how much better my life has become since that commissioning.

The good thing that came from the attack of the Heresy Hunters was that it caused me to shift my focus and begin to prepare to take the good news of The Kingdom outside of the current American evangelical church realm of which I had been a part for over a decade.

I had concluded that I would take The Kingdom message back into the arts and entertainment mountain through some connections that I still held in the music scene. When unexpectedly, a "remantling" would shift the direction of my life and take me from that small town in the Panhandle of Texas, and place me in rooms with the most powerful people on Earth, enabling me to experience the dream that I was just beginning to realize in my heart, the dream of being a voice for The Kingdom at the tables where the cultures of nations are shaped.

CHAPTER 10
REMANTLED FOR GOVERNMENT

A small but mighty gathering of Kingdom believers had begun to brave the local criticism of my "heretical belief systems," and met regularly as I continued to be faithful to my directive to feed the few "Kingdom hungry" individuals in my small corner of the Bible Belt. This Kingdom movement began by meeting in homes, then we utilized a local community center once a month. We eventually rented a facility from a kind Christian businessman from the area, whom I had a great past relationship with. He offered me a discounted rate so we would have a place to meet on a regular basis.

At one of our gatherings, a guest prophet from out of town called me out and spoke a phrase that took me completely off guard. "Dubb, God is re-mantling you for government."

Although this commissioning seemed completely out of left field, and coupled with the fact that I knew very little about government, something in my spirit jumped at the words, and I immediately agreed to receive the assignment.

This prophetic word became the catalyst for a series of enlightening conversations between myself and Holy Spirit, through which I began to see that I was better equipped for this assignment than I thought.

Holy Spirit first brought my attention to the fact that, for years, I had been intentionally becoming familiar with God's way of doing government. Because The Kingdom, in fact, while familial in nature, is actually governmental in structure. Meaning, The Kingdom consists of a royal family who are meant to rule and reign here on earth.

Indeed, Jesus did not come to bring a religion but a government! As Isaiah makes quite clear in Isaiah 9:6-7a, "For unto us a Child is born, unto us a Son is given; and the government will be upon His shoulder. And His name will be called Wonderful, Counselor, Mighty God, Everlasting Father, Prince of Peace. Of the increase of His government and peace, there will be no end..." (NKJV)

Religion is mankind's desperate attempt to meet God, whereas, The Kingdom is the result of God meeting humanity in all of mankind's fallenness and brokenness; and then, redeeming, reconciling, and reestablishing him in his original place as a representative of governmental authority from Heaven on Earth.

"It's simple," Holy Spirit reassured me. "You may not know the governments of man, but you know My government very well. Just take whatever government man hands to you and shift it to align with My way of doing government."

This made sense, and I began to pray for doors to open for me to speak into government. The opportunity came more quicky than I had expected when within a few months of delivering the directional, destiny word, this same prophet (who still serves as a prophet to the first family of an African nation) called me and said, "Get your passport and pack your suits. I'm taking you to Africa with me to meet with the first family.

This was exciting and surreal, and yet, I had one small problem. I did not own any suits. I did, however, own a sweet, flat black, '79 Monte Carlo lowrider, equipped with a radical airbag suspension system. So, with a heavy heart, I concluded that this would be the sacrifice that would be made to equip myself for the next season. I sold the lowrider, procured my passport, and after purchasing suits and roundtrip tickets to Africa, I was ready for my first governmental adventure.

The people of this specific nation love and honor the prophet whom I was accompanying, and on my first international, governmental trip, I was more than happy to ride his coattails as they rolled out the red carpet for him. Armed, presidential escorts were our mode of transportation. We stayed in fenced-in compounds, and a ridiculous number of servants waited on our every need.

If the move from Oak Cliff to Amarillo had been a culture shock, my first experience with the top tier of a nation's government was just as shocking. I found myself at the table with the Minister of Tourism, the Minister of Agriculture, and various presidential cabinet and first family members, where I sat quietly in my new suit, determined to adhere to the wisdom of Abraham Lincoln. "It is better to remain silent and be thought a fool than to speak and remove all doubt." [2]

Throughout the trip, I was acutely aware of unusual things going on. First, I began to have frequent experiences of déjà vu, a phenomenon

---

[2] (Quote Investigator 2010)

that I had previously concluded (based on some thoughts from Lance) was evidence of one catching up with where God had already placed one's face in the future. This concept is seen in scripture in Acts 9, when on the heels of Saul's Damascus Road experience, God comes to Ananias and tells him that Saul has already seen his face. When Ananias catches up in the physical to the place where God had placed his face in the future, it unlocks both sight and identity, and we see "Blind Saul" become "Seeing Paul." And so it should be with us; as we arrive in moments of convergence in walking out our purpose and destiny, those around us should be able to see more clearly what should be done, as well as step into a deeper level of understanding about who they are in the eyes of their Father. All that being said, I welcomed the déjà vu as God's confirmation that I was right where I was supposed to be in that moment of my life.

Secondly, my prophetic gifting went through the roof; however, I did not say anything about the fact that, with an unusual level of clarity and detail, I was hearing prophetic strategies for almost every issue that was discussed. I would later learn, from a future mentor, Dano McCollam, that I was experiencing what it is like to encounter one's *metron of kanon* (in the Greek), or "measure of rule" as described by Paul in 2 Corinthians 10. "Measure of rule" is a sovereignly, predetermined area of authority that one is meant to influence. In the words of Dano, "Your prophetic gifting works all the time, everywhere, with everybody. But there is a specific time, in a specific place, with a specific people group where your prophetic gifting will operate at another level. This is an indicator that you have found your *metron*." And I had certainly found mine.

Finally, it was painfully obvious to me that I did not have a grasp or understanding of how high levels of global government worked. I was completely ignorant of the order and traditions of seating arrangements, titles, and the protocols necessary for greeting varying levels of government officials. Although I had already begun to intentionally work on increasing my personal levels of self-awareness and emotional intelligence as a necessary component of kingship, I could see that for my personal assignment, cultural and situational awareness would need to be added to my skillset.

After this first foray into the world of global government, I sought out statesman training, which I was able to secure from an ambassador of another African country, who just happened to be a Kingdom man. It was here that I pulled on all his knowledge and vast experience concerning how to move appropriately in governmental circles of this level, and more importantly, the process of how to research a nation before going in so as to be equipped with knowledge of the government-specific protocol, and the cultural understanding to be able to move effectively and inoffensively within any given nation.

At the conclusion of my six months of training, he looked at me and said, "You know, Dubb, if you really want to impact global government for The Kingdom, you must select a global issue, discover The Kingdom solution, and present it on a covert platform."

This resonated deeply with me. I had already figured out that truth is truth, even when it is not wearing a Jesus t-shirt. I knew that truth is not a thing but is actually the Person of Jesus Christ (John 14:6), and when Truth is released into a situation, Truth is going to do what Truth does, and that is make people free (John 8:32).

There was just one more question before I went to work, "Ambassador, how does one pick the issue?" I asked.

"What makes you angry?" he responded.

I did not even have to think. "Fatherlessness," I stated emphatically.

"That is most certainly a global issue," my friend the ambassador responded. "Discover the Kingdom solution; make it available on a covert platform, and that will open all the doors to you," he reiterated.

I immediately went to work, but not even the assignment's deep resonance with my spirit could clue me in to just how accurately he had spoken concerning the results of this assignment, especially as to how quickly those doors would open all the way to the very top of global government over the next year.

CHAPTER 11
FATHERS ADD VALUE

For my covert platform, I settled on the name, "Fathers Add Value," and proceeded to craft a strategy to combat the results of fatherlessness. I designed a finely tuned speech around the subject to be delivered in the style of a statesman, produced a small booklet outlining the principles laid out in the speech, and launched a website as a platform that would both display the concept and serve as a vehicle for booking speaking engagements on the topic.

The strategy was simple—make people aware of those around them who are fatherless, regardless of age; realize that said individuals have to some degree experienced lack in the areas of provision, protection, and promotion; recognize that, while the ability to provide for someone is limited by one's personal resources and that one's ability to protect another is limited by proximity, the ability to promote or empower someone is an unlimited commodity.

The best way to empower an individual resulting in their promotion can be produced by the following three steps:

Trust – Choose to trust the individual and their potential before they deserve it.

Encourage – Be intentional to encourage the individual by pointing out their greatness.

Champion – Leverage whatever platform you have on behalf of the individual in question and present him or her to the world in a positive light.

I had simply put on paper the process that I had personally experienced and benefited from in my interactions with Mark. Now, to those of us who are familiar with The Kingdom and the nature of God, this strategy may seem relatively simple and a somewhat common-sense process. However, the world received this concept with a standing ovation, and within just six months of launching Fathers Add Value, I experienced rapid accelera-tion and went from being asked to speak at local governmental meetings, to being invited to Washington, D.C. as a resource to a representa-tive from a nation which had survived an AIDS epidemic and a genocide, leaving a staggering percentage of the population without fathers present in the home.

As I arrived for this divine appointment in the organization's board room on Pennsylvania Avenue, mere blocks from the White House, I was warmly greeted by the vice president and the CFO of the organization, brothers whom I had previously met at various governmental functions.

I took a seat at the end of the table and watched as the room slowly filled with representatives of different nations, who sat along one side of the long table, bringing some of the problematic issues of their individual nations in the hope of finding their solutions. Seated opposite these representatives were business owners whose companies produced products and processes that might possibly serve as solutions for the issues at hand.

When everyone had been seated, the chairman, a gregarious, congenial individual who had a long track record of integrity and connections in the elite circles of Washington D.C. politics, called the meeting to order.

He invited the representative from the first country to share about the issue facing his nation, and as the man began to speak, the door behind him opened and a late comer entered the room. I could tell by the cut and the fabric of the gentleman's suit that he was an official of another country, and as all the seats were taken, I immediately got up and offered him my chair, which he graciously accepted. Upon observing my small but courteous gesture, the CFO seated at the head of the table stood up and motioned for me to take his seat. I remember thinking, *I've read about this in the Bible*, referencing Jesus' instruction in Luke 14:10, "But when you are invited, go and sit down in the lowest place, so that when he who invited you comes, he may say to you, 'Friend, go up higher.' Then you will have glory in the presence of those who sit at the table with you." (NKJV)

This brief seating exchange strategically repositioned me so that instead of being one of the first to speak, I would quite literally be last, and I was now seated next to the chairman of the organization. From my newly bestowed position of honor, I listened intently as the representatives from the different nations shared the issues they had come to present, and with equal interest, listened to the strategies and solutions presented by the business owners seated on the other side of the table.

During these exchanges, I experienced the same phenomenon as I had in Africa—prophetic strategies highlighting missing pieces that needed to be partnered with the practical solutions being presented at the table. I knew that if I were to share these thoughts, they would need to be delivered in secular language in order to be received.

I had not the slightest clue as to the religious beliefs of the governmental representatives at the table, and my mind raced feverishly, working to pull the "Christian-ese" out of what I had heard. I needed to replace the usual prophetic language that I had grown accustomed to using in church with phrases that someone with no concept of Who God was or of His interest in being involved in their nations could easily understand, a process that I now call verbal engineering.

Finally, the chairman of the hosting organization turned to me and asked if I was ready to speak on the solution I had brought to the nation crippled by fatherlessness. "I am," I replied, "but first, may I speak to a couple of the other topics that have been brought to the table?"

I could tell the chairman was somewhat surprised, but he graciously gave me the floor. I quickly and covertly shared the strategies received from Holy Spirit, which would bring a higher level of impact and sustainability when added to the practical solution already presented at the table. To my great relief, my words were well received, invoking follow up questions from both individuals as they added the strategies to the notes they had already taken.

After that exchange, I proceeded with my scheduled, "Fathers Add Value" presentation, which was also met with approval. The meeting drew to a close, and everyone at the table considered it a success on all accounts.

As I walked out the door beside the vice president, he cocked his head and asked me, "Where did that extra input come from?" Now at this point, I knew this gentleman was a believer; however, in our brief conversations I had not perceived an especially high value for things from the charismatic streams.

Here goes nothing, I thought to myself, not knowing what his reaction might be. "Well man, that's the prophetic," I said, and then proceeded to share with him what I had actually heard and how I had verbally engineered the prophetic strategy into what he had heard me deliver.

He nodded and was silent for a minute, and then looked back at me inquisitively. "Can you do that all the time?" he queried.

I inwardly sighed in relief as I responded with all the confidence I could muster, "I think so?"

This was the beginning of a close friendship and a continued working relationship with all three of these gentlemen that continues to this day. And unexpectedly, it was through these three relationships that the rest of the doors would open on my way to the level of global governmental access and influence that I currently enjoy.

*The ability to promote or empower
someone is an unlimited commodity.*

CHAPTER 12
PLACE OF PAIN, PLACE OF REIGN

The late, great Kim Clement made the statement that, "Your place of pain shall become your place of reign."[3] By this time, I may have discovered my *metron of kanon*, my measure of rule, but I had no idea how these doors that were opening were intrinsically tied to the redemption of my entire life's story.

For the next few years, I continued to walk through every open door that presented itself into engagement with government. I continued to discover, learn, and perfect the art of implementing the prophetic gift covertly, on behalf of government officials in various nations, that it might make the goodness of God available to the people under their purview. I call this craft, "the strategies of Heaven, delivered in the style of kings, all for the sake of the people."

---

[3] (Clement 2008)

During this time, one of the places in government where I had the honor to speak was with the mayor of the city where I resided, a connection made by a good friend and fellow local prophet. The mayor was a believer, and quite prophetic herself; although, I do not know that she would have called it that. In one of our meetings, I walked in, and, after initial greetings and pleasantries, she pushed her prayer journal across the desk and pointed at a phrase that she had written there, "Song of the City."

"I was praying, and The Lord impressed upon me that there is a song of the city, and if we find it and sing it, that some things will shift in our region," she stated matter-of-factly.

Now, to some this may sound like a strange idea, but it immediately made sense to me as I had been following the teachings of Dan McCollam, who heads up a ministry called "Sounds of the Nations." This ministry carries the mandate to, "raise up musicianaries in nations to hear and release the song of the Lord through the sound of the people."

If this man can find the sound of a nation, I thought to myself, *finding the song of a city should be child's play.* Luckily, some of my work in Washington D.C. had been with a colleague who was good friends with Dano, so I reached out to my associate and asked him to put me in touch with him, which he did.

After giving me the contact information for Sounds of the Nations' North American director, Dano had a question for me, "So, tell me about how you are operating prophetically in government?"

I shared with him a little of my journey, some of the projects I was working on, and some of my processes surrounding the crucial art of verbal engineering which had proved to be one of the greatest keys in the level of impact that I was experiencing. Upon the conclusion of my story, Dano was kind enough to extend me an invitation to come and share at a round table of prophets that were meeting at The Mission Church in Vacaville, California, in just a few months.

I accepted enthusiastically, and before I knew it, I found myself seated in a room where, for the first time, I was surrounded by people like myself. There were prophets and apostles, walking in Kingdom revelation and passionate about seeing revival. And they also wanted a Kingdom reformation to touch the earth and change every aspect of culture. It was at this meeting that I found my tribe, and my season of feeling alone in this Kingdom journey would come to an end.

Not long after the meeting began, I was asked to come to the front and share what I was doing. I eagerly took the opportunity to share one of my favorite stories in which I heard a prophetic strategy, verbally engineered it, and shared it in my familiar covert fashion with a governmental official who listened with great interest. As is customary when sharing testimonies concerning governmental interaction, I intentionally left the name of the official and even the name of the country out of the story. In addition, no one in the room was aware of my past, much less my family history to which I had made no reference, but remember, I was in a room full of prophets. Apparently, I did not have to say the name of the country, Guyana, which was the central focus of my story for some of them to pick up on it prophetically.

At the conclusion of my story, a prophet named Kim Maas stood up and spoke from the back of the room, "The Lord is sending you to Guyana, they have just found oil and are seeking wisdom." Her next few words stunned me and triggered a phrase from the Lord that would be the most powerful thing I had ever heard. She continued, "America has made Guyana famous worldwide for a cult of death, and the Lord is sending you there to give them a clean slate."

To this day, I am not sure if she said anything else after those words because the next thing that I heard was my heavenly Father's voice speaking to me more clearly than I had ever heard Him in my entire life, words that I will remember as long as I live. "Son, as you know what it is to bear the soul-wound of a father who was a cult leader, I am now sending you to a nation that bears the soul-wound of a cult in order to father it back into its original design."

The words rang over and over in my head and settled deeper and deeper into my spirit than anything I had ever experienced. I graciously thanked Kim for her prophetic word, expressed that I had fully received it, and foggily found my way back to my seat. Afterward, Kim came up to me and handed me her business card that I carry in my wallet to this day; it is white and green and bears the image of a dragonfly prominently displayed on the front.

A few months later, I received a call from my good friend, the vice president of the organization with which I continue to work (who, for the rest of this story, I will refer to as the VP).

"We've got some meetings lined up in Guyana and Suriname here in a couple of weeks, and I want you to go with me."

Laughing on the inside, I immediately agreed to accompany him. "I see you, Lord," I said as I ended the call. If this progression of events had not already been so clearly marked with the supernatural fingerprints of God's redemption, the invitation to Guyana and its timing would have been unbelievable.

I immediately ramped up the intensity of my already in progress research concerning all things Guyana, with a special emphasis on Jim Jones and the Jonestown Massacre. Imagine my surprise when a week later the VP called me back, "Hey man, Guyana fell through, looks like we'll just be going to Suriname."

However, I knew that I was on assignment, and not just any assignment—a destiny assignment. "Well," I replied, "I'm going to Guyana, and I'll meet you in Suriname."

There was a long pause on the other end, and from several states away I could sense the VP's confusion mixed with curiosity. "Why?" the question finally came. By this time, our friendship had grown, and through many conversations, we had come to share the same passion for The Kingdom and were very much on the same page.

"Well, Bro," I responded, "I was going to wait to tell you face-to-face but this is what is happening." I laid out all the details leading up to my current life's assignment, at the end of which the VP summed up how he felt about the whole situation with the phrase, "Shoot, Bro, I'm going with you to Guyana."

Two weeks later, we found ourselves on a flight headed to the nation who held the keys to the redemption of my life's story as much as I held the keys to hers. I sat on the plane a few rows up from my friend, the VP, reviewing and fine-tuning the prophetic declaration that I intended to release over the nation of Guyana. All at once, my shuffled worship playlist began to play The Helsers' song, "Lazarus." As the song began to play, it was as if I could hear the nation of Guyana herself singing to me:

You stood outside my grave
With tears still on Your face
I heard You say my name
My night was turned to day
You came, I knew that You would come
You sang, My heart it woke up
I'm not afraid, I see Your face, I am alive
You came, I knew that You would come[4]

---

[4] (Bethel Music 2016)

In that moment, the weightiness of my assignment gripped my heart in a whole new way; I was overcome with emotion and humbled at the profound value of my assignment. Much to the chagrin of the stranger seated next to the window in my row, I began to weep. The man promptly pretended to go to sleep to avoid the awkwardness to which I was unintentionally subjecting him.

After our arrival in Guyana, as the VP and I navigated our way through the protocols and procedures that come with entering another nation and making our way to the hotel, I was struck by the prominence of the late 90s R&B and HipHop music playing everywhere we went. It was like stepping back in time into one of my favorite eras of music. *I could get use to this!*

Upon arriving at the hotel, I could not wait to step out on the balcony of our high-rise accommodations. For the first time, I was able to see the capital of this beautiful nation sprawled out below me from a bird's eye view.

I pulled out my leatherbound journal and slowly and intentionally spoke out the carefully wordsmithed prophetic declaration that I had penned there. I repented on behalf of my native nation for what Jim Jones, an American, had done to the global reputation of this country, and then I proceeded to call out all her identity, greatness, and potential in the same way that I spoke to my daughter as I tucked her into bed at night.

Once this was done, I felt a rush of joy, and once again I heard Father's voice as He spoke to me saying, "Well done, son. She has a clean state." In that moment, I realized my favorite quote from Kim Clement had just been proven true in my life. My place of pain had indeed become my place of reign in the Kingdom.

*"Your place of pain shall
become your place of reign."*

CHAPTER 13
CONFIRMATION AND
CREDENTIALS

After this encounter, the VP and I headed downstairs for dinner at the hotel's Japanese steakhouse, on the ground floor level. As we pulled our chairs up to the table, I could not believe my ears. After hearing six hours of late 90s R&B and HipHop, George Strait's "Amarillo by Morning" came on over the radio. I grabbed the VP's arm. "Do you hear what is playing right now?" I asked.

His eyes grew wide as he put two and two together. "The Lord is with us," he said solemnly. Just as I had experienced the nation calling out to me on the flight over, it was as if the country of Guyana was now thanking me for what I had brought to its shores, by singing the song of the city from which I had come.

Another American was seated at the same table, a wealthy businessman who struck up a conversation with us. We really seemed to hit it off, a fact that was confirmed at the close of the night when he invited us to attend a party hosted by the US Embassy, in honor of the US Ambassador to Guyana, who was finishing his appointment and would be heading home the next month. Many governmental officials would be in attendance to honor his service, including the president of Guyana himself. "I have a couple of extra tickets; would you gentleman like to attend?" he offered. I, for one, did not have to think twice—*metron* baby!

"Absolutely!" I accepted as calmly as I could.

The next night found us suited up, cufflinks and all, walking through security and into the ballroom that had been rented by the embassy where we bumped elbows with dignitaries, high-ranking military officers, and other individuals of im-portance. For an hour or two, we wandered in and out of conversations, looking for impactful connec-tions for possible new ventures.

Nearing the end of the night, President David Granger took the stage, and after making a heartfelt speech recognizing the US Ambassa-dor's work over the last several years, he made his way down off the platform to mingle graciously with the crowd, and just so happened to walk in the direction of the part of the crowd where the VP and I stood.

After a brief introduction and engagement, the night culminated in plans for us to meet the next morning with the Vice President of Guyana and another local statesman who had been in a couple of our D.C. meetings in the past. The Vice President's main concern and focus was, just as Kim Maas had prophesied, the recent discovery of oil right off the coast, and his desire for the indigenous people to not be left out of the windfall of wealth coming to the nation as a whole.

The next evening after our meeting, the VP and I rushed back to the hotel to gather our belongings and head to the airport for the quick jump over to the neighboring country of Suriname where our business would continue.

As we wheeled our luggage out and turned to start down the long hallway toward the elevators, I looked down just in time to avoid stepping on a dragonfly, resting on the floor directly outside my door. I grabbed my friend by the arm and pointed excitedly, "Look!" He was clearly confused by my excitement until I pulled Kim's card from my wallet and showed him the dragonfly logo and then pointed back down toward a dead ringer.

As he was hit with the realization of what I had recognized, the VP raised his eyebrows. "The Lord is with us," he stated for the second time that trip.

Flying back to the states after our time in Suriname, it would be safe to say that I was on cloud nine, but the VP had one more surprise up his sleeve, "Hey man, we are going to swing by the U.N. on the way home and debrief with a few of our colleagues." Per usual, I was "up for it."

Walking the halls of the United Nations was a surreal experience. I had already concluded that despite brief, yet impactful moments in which I had gotten to show up and make a difference in our own federal government, that the majority of my favor and calling lay with global government. As I moved in and out of different rooms, this was further confirmed by an almost continuous feeling of déjà vu.

Remarkably, I met several people who had worked with Dr. Myles Munroe in the past and were undeniably working within the U.N. on purpose, for purpose. They were and are there on a Kingdom mission, to infiltrate the machine that the U.N. is, and to influence it to begin to accomplish the agenda of The Kingdom! As Jesus said in Matthew 13:33 (NLT), "The Kingdom of Heaven is like the yeast a woman used in making bread. Even though she put only a little yeast in three measures of flour, it permeated every part of the dough." You see, the yeast is in the dough, and the funny thing about that is once the yeast is in the dough, you cannot get it out!

As I travel today, I am often amused by the conceptions that many churches have surrounding the U.N. and its ultimate purpose and destiny. Sometimes, I will jack with the crowd, and after my introduction, I will start talking about how there is an agenda out there at work to see a one world government take preeminence over the whole earth. Some will lean in with bated breath, and I can hear them saying to themselves, "I knew it!"

Then I burst their bubble with the statement, "It's called The Kingdom!" From there, I proceed to point them to scripture after scripture, containing the truth that The Kingdom wins, not some mythical half man, half Satan creature and his henchmen of demonic cohorts, marching under the banner of a new world order, but I digress. That is another book for another day.

It was in one of those meetings during my first U.N. experience that the connections were established that would result in my being credentialed through an NGO, non-governmental organization, that carries ECOSOC status within the U.N. These credentials have allowed me to carry my own grounds access card to the U.N.'s New York facility for the last few years.

All in all, it was a pretty good trip in my book. It is amazing what doors Father will open for those who take the development of their kingship seriously. It is as if Jesus knew what He was talking about when He stated that if we would seek first The Kingdom, that all things would be added to us. (Matthew 6:33)

The culmination of that whole trip occurred several months later as I was mindlessly scrolling through Facebook™ to unwind from the day. A post from my friend, the ambassador who had provided my statesman training, caught my eye. In the picture, he stood next to, of all people, the Vice President of Guyana receiving a gift, but it was the accompanying quote that probably meant just a little more to me than anybody else who read it that day. *"Vice President of Indigenous Affairs of the Republic of Guyana, presents visiting ambassador with a commemorative painting of their fifty years of independence, stating that the publicity that the ambassador has brought to their country is responsible for putting his nation on the world's map in a positive light."*

I turned my phone off and lay back, closing my eyes. Sometimes, the tangibility of what one does or accomplishes "in the spirit" is arguable, even inside of said individual's head, but this was all the external confirmation that I would ever need as to the validity and purpose of the clean slate that it had been my honor to provide to Guyana on that sweltering hot day, standing on the balcony of the Ramada Princess, overlooking the capital city.

In that moment, everything was worth it—my crazy past, the family cult, and the spiritual abuse. I realized that I would honestly go through it all again just to become the one who bore the authority in the spirit to free a nation from the marks of like bondage and destruction so that she could be known for her original intent and continue walking in the fulfillment of the purpose and destiny for which she was designed.

Once the yeast is in the dough, you cannot get it out!

CHAPTER 14
SCHOOL OF KINGDOM

After that night, I was quite content to do my thing, operating as a covert prophet in the highest levels of global government. But not too long after I began to engage the U.N., as I sat at lunch with Dano and a few other close Kingdom comrades, he leaned back in his chair and casually asked a question that would unlock the next assignment in my life.

"You know, Dubb," he started in his usual laid-back style of communication, "what you do to advance The Kingdom in government is really cool but let me ask you a question. Would you rather sit with a king of the earth once a week, or raise up thousands who sit with kings daily?"

If you have gotten any sort of a feel for me through this story, by now I am sure that you can guess my response. I am all for impact and literally changing the world. "No question," I replied, "raise up thousands who sit with kings daily."

"Awesome," Dano replied casually. "Then you should start a school and teach people what you know and how to do what you do." With that, he turned his attention back to his lunch.

It never ceases to amaze me how impactful and destiny-laden a few words can be when they are spoken from a right heart at the right time.

Three years later at the time of this writing, School of Kingdom U.S. currently has 321 students deeply engaged in its ten-month journey. In addition, both School of Kingdom Australia, and School of Kingdom South Africa are off to an exciting start, enjoying their first year of existence.

School of Kingdom exists to Discover, Develop and Deploy Prophetic Kingdom Reformers. These are people who are passionate about seeing The Kingdom advance powerfully in their lifetimes. These are people who want to be intentional to develop their prophetic gift into a practical skill. These are people who believe that the Great Commission carries within it a mandate for the sons and daughters of God to show up powerfully within the systems of the world, carrying the strategies of Heaven until we see the kingdoms of this world become The Kingdom of our God. If this sounds like you, I would like to invite you to visit schoolofkingdom.com.

I will leave you with this; if you need hope for our world, you can have some of mine. I have tapped into an unlimited supply. I am convinced of and have committed my life to believing the following truths:

1. That we have a good, kind, and loving heavenly Father who has designed each one of us with a unique Identity, Purpose, and Destiny.

2. That we belong to The King of kings, King Jesus, who has not only reconciled *us* back to the waiting, loving arms of our Father, but also redeemed us back to our original value and repositioned us as the kings of the earth mentioned in scripture here and now.

3. That the Person of Holy Spirit has joyfully chosen to take up residence within us, carrying all the gifts, graces, and supernatural power that we need in order to change the world.

These truths are enough for me and my family to live out purposeful, joy-filled lives, and The Kingdom is available to all. Wherever you start—hood, cult, new age, addiction, institution, suburb, corporate office, cubicle, emerging nation, or mansion in Beverly Hills—the invitation to rule and reign in The Kingdom is waiting for you.

To The King,

Dubb Alexander

BIBLIOGRAPHY

Bethel Music. 2016. *You Came (Lazarus).* Comps.
    Melissa Helser, John Helser and Ed Cash.
Clement, Kim. 2008. *Elijah List - Kim Clement:
    "God's Changing Our Whole Structure, Our
    Whole Economy. There is an Economy of
    Grace!* May 21. Accessed August 2021.
    http://www.elijahlist.com/words/display_wor
    ds/6470.
Munroe, Dr. Myles. 2013. *Rediscovering the
    Kingdom Expanded Edition: Ancient Hope
    for Our 21st Century World.* Destiny Image
    Publishers; Expanded ed. edition.
Quote Investigator. 2010. May 17. Accessed
    August 2021.
    https://quoteinvestigator.com/2010/05/17/re
    main-silent/.

ABOUT THE AUTHOR

Dubb Alexander advances The Kingdom as a Global Statesman, leveraging his United Nations access to bring prophetic strategies to heads of state around the world. When he is not traveling internationally, Dubb can be found equipping Prophetic Kingdom Reformers through his online school, "School of Kingdom," or sharing the platform alongside other Kingdom Generals at various conferences and training events. Dubb resides in Amarillo, Texas, with his beautiful wife, Beth, and their daughter, Cinda.

KINGDOM CONNECTION

	Website	www.schoolofkingdom.com
	Facebook	facebook.com/schoolofkingdom
	Instagram	@schoolofkingdom
	YouTube	youtube.com/c/schoolofkingdom

Made in the USA
Coppell, TX
22 October 2021

64515361R00083